Reach the Top in Finance

D0886152

Reach the Top in Finance

The ambitious accountant's guide to career success

By Sally Percy

Bloomsbury Business
An imprint of Bloomsbury Publishing Plc

B L O O M S B U R Y
LONDON · OXFORD · NEW YORK · NEW DELHI · SYDNEY

Bloomsbury Business
An imprint of Bloomsbury Publishing Plc

50 Bedford Square	1385 Broadway
London	New York
WC1B 3DP	NY 10018
UK	USA

www.bloomsbury.com

BLOOMSBURY and the Diana logo are trademarks of Bloomsbury Publishing Plc

First published 2017

© Sally Percy, 2017

Sally Percy has asserted her right under the Copyright, Designs and
Patents Act, 1988, to be identified as Author of this work.

All rights reserved. No part of this publication may be reproduced or
transmitted in any form or by any means, electronic or mechanical,
including photocopying, recording, or any information storage or retrieval
system, without prior permission in writing from the publishers.

No responsibility for loss caused to any individual or organization acting
on or refraining from action as a result of the material in this publication
can be accepted by Bloomsbury or the author.

British Library Cataloguing-in-Publication Data
A catalogue record for this book is available from the British Library.

ISBN: PB: 978-1-4729-3810-7
ePDF: 978-1-4729-3808-4
ePub: 978-1-4729-3811-4

Library of Congress Cataloging-in-Publication Data
A catalog record for this book is available from the Library of Congress.

Cover design by Eleanor Rose
Cover image © Getty Images

Typeset by Deanta Global Publishing Services, Chennai, India
Printed and bound in Great Britain

Contents

Foreword

If you want a peaceful life on a sun lounger, do not be a CFO.

Julie Brown, CFO, Smith & Nephew

Like so many creative endeavours, this book began with a question: what does it take to get to the very top of the finance profession?

Or, more precisely, who do you need to be to become one of those rare individuals with a seven-figure salary who works as a finance leader in an organization that employs tens of thousands of people across the globe? How do you deal with the stress and pressure of a job like that – the hours, the travel and the knowledge that the decisions you take will affect the livelihoods of so many?

What are the personal attributes and skills that you need in order to fulfil your professional role as a linchpin of the capital markets? How can you give confidence to investors and a range of other stakeholders that the financial statements of the business that you help to run – or audit – can be relied on and that you're not actually presiding over what is potentially the next major corporate collapse?

Finally, are finance leaders born – or are they made?

It is virtually impossible to overstate the sheer level of responsibility that comes with holding a very senior role in finance. One of the people interviewed for this book presides over a finance function that numbers more than 4,000 people globally. Another found out on his first day as a group finance director that the company was less than a fortnight away from collapsing into administration. When you're a CFO, both your successes and your failures can be very public; your reputation is always on the line and a bad slip-up could mean an abrupt end to your previously glittering career. While the rewards on offer can be substantial, there is no doubt that at its highest levels, the world of finance can be mildly hair-raising at best and unthinkably brutal at worst.

As a journalist, I have had the privilege of getting to meet – and interview – some of the most successful people in the finance profession over the years. I have also been fortunate enough to be able to talk to them for this book. What I have learned is that as with most careers, there is no one 'right' path that you can follow to get to the top in finance. The path that you take will depend on your own personal ambitions and interests, your sector, your market, whether you work in practice or industry, your gender, your background and, of course, your own personal definition of success.

So while this book does not claim that there is only one route to the top, it does use the expert knowledge and personal reflections of some very senior finance professionals to offer some important career strategies.

It goes, without saying, that this book would not have been possible without the help of the inspiring and talented finance leaders listed below, who gave up some of their precious time to explain just what it takes to succeed in finance. I am immensely grateful to them. Their job titles are those they held at the time that they were interviewed for the book:

- Lucinda Bell, CFO, British Land
- Stephen Billingham, chair, Anglian Water, Punch Taverns and Urenco; and non-executive director, Balfour Beatty
- Andrew Bonfield, finance director, National Grid
- Julie Brown, CFO, Smith & Nephew
- Rachel Campbell, global head of people, performance and culture, KPMG International
- Paul Donofrio, CFO, Bank of America
- Ronan Dunne, CEO, Telefónica UK
- Peter Hargreaves, founder, Hargreaves Lansdown
- Ian Kenyon, CFO, Cancer Research UK
- Scott Longhurst, group finance director, Anglian Water
- Geraldine Matchett, CFO, Royal DSM
- Jack McGinnis, CFO, ManpowerGroup
- Rich Neal, CEO, MyWorkpapers
- Sacha Romanovitch, CEO, Grant Thornton UK
- Brad Sugars, founder, ActionCOACH
- Julie Teigland, regional managing partner – Germany, Switzerland and Austria, EY
- David Tilston, former CFO of Innovia Group

Further thanks must go to the following professionals for the invaluable perspectives that they brought to this book:

- Mark Freebairn, partner and head of the financial management practice, Odgers Berndtson
- Sharron Gunn, executive director, members, commercial & shared services, Institute of Chartered Accountants in England and Wales
- Lydia Lamdin, head of professional development, Institute of Chartered Accountants in England and Wales
- Jonathan Ng, executive director, qualification and education, Hong Kong Institute of Certified Public Accountants
- Rohit Talwar, CEO, Fast Future Research
- Karen Young, director, Hays Senior Finance

I would also like to thank Bloomsbury for giving me the opportunity to write this book and for supporting the concept so enthusiastically, as well as Parag Prasad of London Business Coaching, who inspired me to write it.

Finally I must thank my husband and children for being so patient with me during the research and writing process. It's finished now!

Introduction

Finance is one of the world's most popular professions for good reason – numbers matter.

Why do they matter? They matter because numbers underpin the stability of our world and they give confidence to all of us that things are going as they should be. Numbers are used to inform everything from the strategy of the world's biggest multinational (Apple – at the time of writing) through to a college student's decision on whether he or she can afford to upgrade his or her smartphone. Get them right and numbers serve as valuable indicators of the health of businesses, governments and individuals. Get them wrong and they can destroy careers, organizations and even lives.

Since the majority of people on this planet want numbers to be right, they need the people who are in charge of producing the numbers to be competent, ethical and reliable. For this reason, there are a host of professional bodies around the world that offer accountancy qualifications to individuals who want to pursue careers in public practice, education, government service, industry and commerce. Each year hundreds of thousands of people around the world enter the finance profession by training with one of these bodies and the majority of them emerge with a qualification that is proof of their ability to prepare a set of financial statements, understand accounting standards, apply tax relief and perhaps audit a company.

These individuals – who are usually bright, ambitious and capable – then go on to develop their careers within the finance profession. Thanks to their expertise and the responsibilities that come with their roles, they are usually well paid compared with peers who work in other professions and some of them will go on to earn six-figure or seven-figure salaries as the CFOs of multinationals or partners at one of the Big Four accountancy firms.

The benefits of a career in finance don't just stop at monetary rewards, however. They also include diversity of work, responsibility and the opportunity to switch between industry sectors. Finance is a truly international career that presents many opportunities for its practitioners to work in a wide variety of locations around the world. Finally, it offers relative job security compared with other occupations.

Those who make it to the most senior levels in finance have jobs that extend far beyond number crunching. In industry, they are typically the right-hand man or woman to the CEO, relied on to help set strategy, manage transformation and IT projects and to reassure investors. So they need to be comfortable interacting with a wide range of stakeholders from shareholders and auditors through to bankers, journalists, customers, suppliers and staff. Not only that, their integrity must be incontestable.

In the large accountancy firms, which are multinational businesses, partners are trusted advisers to their clients, helping to solve difficult business problems. They are also sales people (who are expected to bring in new business to the firm), marketers (who are expected to raise the profile of the firm in the marketplace), innovators (who create new products and services), and leaders of large numbers of people. PwC, which is just one of the so-called Big Four professional services firms, employs over 200,000 people globally.

In the public sector, finance professionals manage some huge budgets (the UK Ministry of Defence has an annual budget of £38bn, for example, while its US counterpart has a budget of $601bn), so they must know how to handle the inevitable scrutiny from politicians and the media that accompanies this.

While finance is undoubtedly a rewarding career at the highest levels, it is a competitive profession and it is tough to reach the top. Therefore, while numbers will always matter greatly, the skills that finance professionals need to enable them to reach their full potential in their careers extend far beyond the technical expertise that they developed during their training.

Ultimately, success means different things to different people. Perhaps you want to climb to the greatest heights of the finance profession as the CFO of a multinational. Perhaps you want to be promoted to partner or finance director in the organization where you currently work. Perhaps you want to land an interesting overseas assignment. Perhaps you want to use your financial background as a basis for running your own business one day. Or perhaps you just want to develop a career that offers you the kind of opportunities that will personally excite you and enable you to reach your full potential.

Regardless of your reasons for choosing to read this book, you will find that it is packed with useful insight – including observations from international finance leaders – on how you can develop the skills that will underpin your personal and professional success in a finance career. Good luck with whatever you choose to do.

Chapter 1

Building your personal brand

The secret to my success

'I'd say strong communication skills, strong rhetorical skills, empathy and good judgement – the ability to be right more often than not. If you're wrong, people will figure it out and won't follow you.'

Paul Donofrio, CFO, Bank of America

The secret to my success

'Authenticity is what sets successful leaders apart. Over a period of time, people need to have the confidence and certainty that what you see is what you get.'

Ronan Dunne, former CEO, Telefónica UK

Regardless of where you are in your finance career, it is never too early – or too late – to start thinking about your personal brand.

Your personal brand is the way in which you present yourself to everyone else in the world – in person, on the telephone, online and in print. Your personal brand encompasses everything that is unique to you – the way you talk, the way you act, the way you dress, the way you engage with others, your personal hobbies and interests, and your own unique strengths and personality traits.

This is a book on succeeding in a career in finance, so why does it start with a chapter on personal brand? It starts that way because if you want to be a finance leader, your personal brand matters – a lot.

We all have a personal brand, but what sets us apart from others during the course of our career is what we do with that brand. Do we assess it, nurture it and actively develop it over time so that it becomes the foundation of our career success or do we ignore it, neglect it and let it meander so that it potentially becomes a cause of professional downfall? People who succeed in a wide variety of occupations usually have a strong personal brand that they have consciously refined during the course of their careers.

Someone who knows the importance of personal brand is Ronan Dunne, an Irish chartered accountant who went on to become CFO and then CEO of telecommunications giant Telefónica UK. He likens himself to 'a 15-year-old kid', describing his brand as being an 'energy giver, curious and engaged'.

He also realized fairly early on in his career that a powerful part of his brand was his natural ability to tell stories. 'I discovered that I could draw on my curiosity and appetite for information by weaving what I had learned into storytelling in a way that helps to bring people on a journey,' he says. 'From a leadership point of view, that is very important.'

Once he had recognized this, he made his commitment to storytelling a very public part of his brand. On the day he was unveiled as CEO, he stood up in front of several hundreds of Telefónica UK's employees and announced that it was his role to be the 'chief cheerleader and chief storyteller' on behalf of the organization. 'It was my personal commitment to aspire to make each employee the success they deserved to be,' he says.

If you are reading this book, the chances are that you are already sensitive to the importance of your personal brand, even if you haven't quite looked at it in that way before. What's more, the fact that you are paying attention to your personal brand shows that you are already demonstrating a very important personal quality that will help to set you apart from your peers as your career progresses – self-awareness.

Why does personal brand matter to finance professionals?

While having a strong personal brand is important for those who want to succeed in their chosen occupation, it is particularly important for finance professionals. That is because finance professionals are entrusted with very serious responsibilities and their slip-ups can have far-reaching consequences. If an organization gets into financial difficulty, employees can lose their jobs and pensions while investors and lenders can lose money. Senior managers can suffer reputational damage and possibly, depending on the circumstances, face criminal charges.

When it comes to money, the stakes are high – hence a company's share price can tumble if a respected CFO announces his or her departure, and international auditing standards now require the names of audit engagement partners to be disclosed.

As a general rule, the world expects all finance professionals to be capable, ethical, honest and professional. And the pressure on them to meet these criteria has intensified since the global financial crisis of 2007–8, which undermined trust in the finance profession. Banks were using complicated financial structures to hide their true exposures and politicians blamed audit firms for giving clean audit reports to banks that then nearly collapsed. While the reputation of the finance profession has recovered since the crisis – both because of the actions of regulators and because of organizations themselves making improvements to restore trust – there remains intense and persistent scrutiny of finance professionals.

'Certain aspects of your personal brand will be key throughout your career,' says David Tilston, a former group CFO of private equity-owned banknote substrate maker Innovia who has also held group finance director roles at publicly listed companies. 'Integrity is probably the most important aspect. You need to be someone who can be trusted by others at all levels within the organisation and outside. You also need to be transparent and able to explain issues in an open way so that people can discuss them candidly. You need to be able to assess risks – without being overly cautious – and to be able to demonstrate good judgment. And as a manager of a large number of people, you need to be able to get the best out of them and to be seen as a strong leader.'

He continues: 'As a senior finance professional, you will be the custodian of a vast amount of data and facts. So it is your job to understand which aspects of the information that you have at your fingertips are relevant to users of accounts and be able to alert them to important trends and highlight the options they may have in terms of taking advantage of opportunities or managing risks.'

The nature of a finance professional's personal brand will vary to some extent according to the nature of his or her current role and what he or she has done in the past. 'So a CFO who is used to supporting fast-growing businesses is likely to need different qualities from a CFO whose expertise lies in turning round businesses,' observes Tilston. 'Also, others will judge you on how you have responded to your mistakes and learned from experience over the course of your career. If you have completely fouled up your relationships with investors and banks, for example, then it might be very difficult to come back.'

Building your brand

While ethics and professionalism are core components of any finance professional's brand, they are far from being the only components. There are a host of other important qualities that a finance professional will be expected to have – from being analytical, diligent, hard-working and punctual through to having the ability to communicate and manage relationships.

In 2016, international accountancy body ACCA identified seven attributes that it saw as being critical to the success of today's accountants.[1] These are technical and ethical competence, problem-solving ability, creativity in terms of using existing knowledge in a new situation to explore potential outcomes and generate ideas, digital awareness, emotional intelligence, an ability to predict future trends and expertise in understanding customer expectations.

Although most finance professionals will share a number of common attributes, we are all different. So the most prominent personal qualities in one finance professional's brand won't necessarily be the same in another's. The key thing with building a personal brand is being true to who you are, however. Trying to present yourself as an outgoing person who can start a conversation with anyone in the business isn't going to work if you're naturally reserved and struggle with small talk. That's why it is important to know yourself when you are trying to develop your brand. Personality assessments such as the DISC or Myers-Briggs tests can help with this. If you search for the terms 'DISC personality test' and 'Myers-Briggs' on the internet, you will be able to find out more.

'You have to be who you are,' says Brad Sugars, founder of global business coaching franchise ActionCOACH. 'If you try to build a brand on someone or something you're not, don't expect a massive level of success. You've got to work out what your strengths are. People will want to work with you based on your strengths, not based on the things you say are your strengths or the things you perceive to be your strengths. Just be yourself and that will be a much better brand than most people create.'

Paul Donofrio, CFO of Bank of America, doesn't particularly identify with the term 'personal brand', but he is conscious of what others expect from a CFO and that is reflected in his own behaviour: 'I think that it is important that you are thoughtful and that other people believe you're thoughtful,' he says. 'They want to know that you've tried to step beyond your biases and that you're using every tool you have to get to the right judgement. It's important for people to believe that you are doing that, because they want to trust your judgement.'

He also emphasizes the importance of integrity (being honest and having strong moral principles), saying: 'I think it's incredibly important that people believe you're going to do the right thing and that you're not going to let things that shouldn't influence you, influence you – for example, your own personal ambitions or a political alliance. You want people to believe you're going to do the right thing because it's the right thing, or because you've come to some judgement based on all that thoughtfulness. Even if a leader makes the wrong decision, you want to believe that the leader believed it was the right decision at the time. People get very frustrated if they think you're doing something for the wrong reason.'

When asked how she would want to appear in front of others, Rachel Campbell, global head of people, performance and culture at KPMG International, says: 'As someone who delivers and who does it in the right way'.

Expounding her point, she adds: 'I want to be seen as someone who can be relied upon, who is effective and who gets things done while acting with integrity. I'm not sure that I've consciously developed that perception of myself, however. The notion that you want to do something in the right way is a deep-seated value that you have, so I think I'm just being conscious of my personal values and how those relate to work.'

The concept of personal brand – or reputation, if you prefer to define it that way – is very significant in the context of financial services, Campbell says. 'I'm an audit partner by background so I'm conscious that I represent the firm in every interaction that I have. I commit to the firm when I sign an audit opinion. It is crucial to be conscious of how clients perceive you and how your team perceives you. I think your personal brand is critically important.'

Sacha Romanovitch, CEO of Grant Thornton UK, also believes that personal brand is critical for finance professionals who hold a client-facing role. 'It comes back to personal qualities,' she says. 'Do they think you're being straight with them and that you have a good command of your subject matter? Do you come across as if you're organised, focused, and paying attention to the right things? That's what's important in terms of credibility.'

She also highlights how appearance can make a big difference to how a finance professional is perceived. 'We work on the basis of "dress for your clients",' she says. 'A lot of our clients are in media and advertising, so when our partners are working with them, they are not necessarily going to go in all fully suited and booted. Equally, if all our clients are suited and booted, then we will dress appropriately. You need to make sure you're focusing on your personal qualities and then presenting yourself in a way that feels respectful to the clients.'

A stand-out brand

What sort of person do you need to be to attract the attention of the finance leaders in your own organization? Donofrio looks out for people who come to 'an independent, thorough conclusion after really thinking hard about all the parts of problem and can then convince me and others that it's the right solution'. He continues: 'Very often, people fall back on what they know, or what their experience is, or what others have done.

But what impresses me is when somebody comes at a goal in a very holistic way, without a lot of prejudices, and has challenged the bias.'

Donofrio's other advice to finance professionals who want to stand out is this: 'Do what you're doing extraordinarily well, try to learn as much as you can in the job you're in, and ask a ton of questions. It's much easier to ask questions when you're early in your career than when you're more senior in your career. Challenge the status quo. Work incredibly hard. Be thoughtful. Do things the way you think is the right way to do them. And show that you can influence people along the way.'

Romanovitch has a number of qualities that she looks out for in more junior members of the firm. 'Curiosity is very important, as is the ability to act not out of self-interest but in the interests of others – your clients, your peers and your stakeholders,' she says. 'You need to have the ability to make sense of what's happening in the world and to possess emotional intelligence. All those qualities are really important.'

Scott Longhurst, group finance director at utility company Anglian Water, says a finance professional who wants to go far needs to have 'the utmost integrity, good commercial acumen and resilience – because it doesn't always go right'. He adds: 'Likeability and charisma are also important and you need to be able to work effectively with other people.'

Mark Freebairn, partner and head of the financial management practice at executive search firm Odgers Berndtson, identifies the signs of a finance professional who is set to excel as 'ambition, drive, an ability to take a risk by putting yourself into some difficult situations with a view to making them better'. He says: 'It's already thinking about how you develop the experience for where you want your career to end up. And having the ability to express how finance adds value to an organisation.'

The value of pragmatism: Julie Teigland

Julie Teigland grew up in Michigan in the United States. An outstanding student, she had her pick of scholarships by the time she reached university age. As she was attracted to the idea of living in Europe, she decided to study in Germany and then in France. In 1990, she started working for Arthur Andersen in Frankfurt, practising in accounting and, later, tax.

She spent over six years doing tax for individuals and companies that had interests in both the United States and Germany. Then, tempted by the prospect of life on the client side, she moved to Berlin to become the European head of finance and accounting for Tishman Speyer Properties, a major real estate property developer. After a few years in that role, she wanted to move back to advisory work, so she rejoined Arthur Andersen and later switched to EY.

Today, Teigland is a senior member of EY's Europe, Middle East, India and Africa (EMEIA) leadership team and deputy regional managing partner for Germany, Switzerland and Austria. While she stands out for being an American woman who holds a leadership role in the European finance profession, she has also differentiated herself by being a role model that other women can relate to. She can be assertive when required, but she is also grounded in her femininity – which sets her apart in a working environment where women frequently feel that they have to adopt certain qualities aligned with masculinity if they want to succeed.

Interestingly, when you ask Teigland how she defines her personal brand, she doesn't focus on how she comes across or what she looks like. Instead, what she says is this: 'I'm extremely pragmatic. And I'm pragmatic because I spent so much time on the client side. When I became head of finance, I had to deal with many advisory firms, including both Andersen and EY. So I developed very strong views about the need for pragmatic, executable advice.'

Her clients really value her pragmatism, Teigland says, because they know that she puts their business first. They also like the fact that she is very clear about the messages that she sends to them. This is just as well because during her career she has had to give some very tough messages to C-suite executives.

Teigland's pragmatism is also evident from the way in which she connects with her internal colleagues at EY. 'If you invite me to a call or a meeting, a) I'm going to participate and b) I'm going to tell you exactly what I think,' she says. 'If you don't want me to say that, don't invite me.'

In the notoriously political environment of a partnership, being pragmatic can be a great help, according to Teigland. 'The only way I can ever come through is by saying exactly what I think,' she says. 'Sometimes that makes me not politically acceptable or politically correct and some people might not like it, but at least you always know where I stand.' 'But,' she adds – and this indicates why her personal brand is so successful, 'I try to say it in a nice way. Also, am I going to say naive things in front of a large audience? Probably not. But will I make sure they get said? Yes, I will.'

While Teigland might define her personal brand as pragmatic, it is clear that she is courageous as well. Many people find it difficult to tell others what they don't want to hear, but it is a necessary part of doing a very senior job.

Hence anyone with ambitions of making it to the top in finance will need to cultivate courage as part of his or her personal brand. And the best way of doing this – for people for whom speaking out does not come naturally – is to do it gradually. Speak out a little first, on subjects that you are very confident addressing, in environments where you feel comfortable, and as time goes on, speak out more and more. Being recognized as someone who is not afraid to front up to bad news or to challenge the thoughts and opinions of others – in a way that comes across as respectful – will be a crucial component of your personal brand as you progress.

Changing your brand

While it usually takes a lot of hard work and a lot of time to build your personal brand, you can unfortunately do a lot of damage to it very quickly thanks to our human tendency to relish the slip-ups of others.

One careless comment, or a misguided email or tweet, can help to put you out of a job – as BP's then chief executive, Tony Hayward, discovered when he complained that he wanted his 'life back' at the time of the massive Gulf of Mexico oil spill in 2010. The comment came after he was thrust into the media spotlight for weeks on end following an explosion on a rig that killed eleven workers and caused the worst oil spill in US history. Just over a month after making the remark, Hayward stood down.

Fortunately, however, Hayward's example is exceptional – and he did find another job with oil exploration company Genel Energy afterwards. If you are concerned about your own personal brand, it is probably far more likely that it needs a little fine-tuning rather than a dramatic overhaul to get your career on track. It also helps to remember that your personal brand is not fixed in stone – it should naturally change and evolve over the course of your career, depending on your experiences and the objectives you set yourself.

'When I was a senior manager, starting my journey coming through to becoming partner, I had an idea that I needed to convey myself in a certain way,' says Sacha Romanovitch. 'I had an idea that I had to be a she-man and I needed to present myself very seriously. I used to straighten my hair and do other things to make it look like I fitted in.'

Romanovitch decided to change tack when she took a year-long sabbatical to go travelling in India. 'Then I realised that what was really important was that I could be me,' she says. 'I decided that my personal brand was to be myself instead of trying to be something that I thought a partner in a professional services firm was supposed to be. When I came back from my sabbatical, I was much more embracing and accepting of who I was and focused on being the best of me as opposed to trying to present myself as I thought I needed to be. That was the transformation for me.'

Effectiveness is an important aspect of Rachel Campbell's personal brand and she says this has evolved over the years. 'I've realised over my career that the less I talk and the more I listen, the more successful I am. To develop my effectiveness, I've explored diverse points of view and deliberately sought out people out who I thought had different points of view from me or who could be potential "derailers." And I've surrounded myself with people who are more talented than me and who will challenge me. Ultimately, I've always tried to understand what might get in the way of success and not shy away from that.'

Marketing your personal brand

There are a number of ways in which you can market yourself to the people who matter – your current line manager, your future line managers, your peers and the wider industry that you work within. The most obvious of these is to do a good job – and, without sounding big-headed – to talk about the fact that you've done a good job.

In addition, you can make use of a variety of other channels to market yourself. So look closely at all your social media profiles – those you use in both your personal and professional lives – and see what kind of impression they give of you. If it's not favourable, then you need to work on those profiles. And even if there is nothing wrong with the profiles, look at how you can improve them. Is your LinkedIn profile comprehensive and up to date, for example? Can you post blogs on the site that demonstrate your expertise? Remember that anyone who meets you in a professional context is likely to Google you these days, so try Googling yourself and see what comes up. If you see things you don't want other people to know about, you need to take action – now. That means deleting any unsuitable posts or photos that you have put up yourself or, where other people have put them up, asking them to remove those posts or photos on your behalf.

As you progress in your career, you can also use the media to build your brand by writing articles for the trade press and doing media training so that you can give comments to journalists.

Ultimately, your personal brand is the most precious professional asset that you have, because it is what makes you unique, so you must protect it and use it wisely. The finance leaders who appear in this book may not always see themselves as having a personal brand as such, but you can be sure that there are some very clear perceptions of them in the marketplace. If you haven't already done so, now is the time to start giving some serious consideration to the strength of your personal brand.

Chapter end

What are the key takeaways from this chapter?

- Personal brand matters a lot to finance professionals because other people rely on them to confirm that numbers are accurate.
- In general, finance professionals are expected to be capable, ethical, honest and professional. The strength of the other qualities that they have will vary according to the individual.
- You need to be authentic and build your personal brand based on what your strengths genuinely are, not what you would like them to be.
- You can use your personal brand to make an impression on senior leaders at an early point in your career.
- You need to actively manage your personal brand and consider the messages that other people get about you through different channels.

Chapter 2

Skills and capabilities

The secret to my success

'According to the people around me, what makes me successful is that I am always authentic. I genuinely care about the outcome, about making projects or strategies successful, and I genuinely care about the people involved.'

Geraldine Matchett,
CFO and management board member, Royal DSM

The secret to my success

'It's probably resilience and the ability to work through potentially difficult situations to achieve successful outcomes. You tend to learn more when the chips are down than when things are going well.'

David Tilston, former CFO, Innovia Group

If you have aspirations of getting to the top in finance, you need to have technical competence in whatever aspect of finance you practise in. So if you want to progress your career in professional services, you will usually need to be competent in audit and/or tax. If you progress your career in the finance functions of organizations, you will need to understand accounts preparation and financial reporting in the context of the relevant accounting standards.

Obviously, there are various corollaries from mainstream finance such as financial planning and analysis, M&A, treasury and insolvency work. While a background in these areas can still be a route to the top in professional services – Ian Powell, PwC's former chairman in the UK, came from a background in insolvency advisory services, for example – the CFOs of large companies have normally had a solid grounding in a technical role at some point during the course of their career.

The importance that is ascribed to technical expertise in the market is clear from the fact that many of the CFOs interviewed for this book had previously served a stint as group financial controller (also known as a group controller in many jurisdictions). For some, it was the natural evolution in their own career progression while others had actually gone out of their way to make sure they gained that experience.

Given the legal obligations that company directors have in most jurisdictions, and the fact that they could go to jail if they fail in those obligations, it is understandable that CFOs want a thorough grounding in the technical aspects of the job. While it is certainly possible for people to reach CFO through routes other than financial accounting, such as tax and treasury, a lack of experience of overseeing the accounts preparation process can be a significant disadvantage, particularly if an individual wants to make an external move rather than progress through the process of internal promotion.

'Without technical competence, nothing else matters,' says Mark Freebairn, partner and head of the financial management practice at executive search firm Odgers Berndtson. 'So if you are a technically incompetent CFO, then no chief executive or audit chair will employ you. The thing that costs a business most is restating its numbers because then it has lost the confidence of its investor base. You can be the most commercial, brightest strategist on the planet, with the nicest personality that everyone wants to follow, but if you are not technically competent enough to guarantee the integrity of the information that the business uses to run itself, you are not a CFO.'

Of course, the reality of CFOs' working lives and the depth and breadth of their leadership and management responsibilities mean that while they do need to be technically competent, they don't usually have the time they may once have had to research accounting standards in depth – especially given that accounting standards are continually changing. As a result, they will often draw on the expertise of their team in technical matters. Nevertheless, they still need to know enough about developments in accounting and external reporting to be able to make judgements about the key risks facing the organization and what information it ought to be communicating, both internally and externally.

Fundamentally, a CFO needs to know enough to be able to ask challenging questions of both his or her team and any external advisers that the organization uses. 'Your role, as a CFO, is to know what expertise you need and where you can get it from,' says Scott Longhurst, group finance director of Anglian Water, who is also responsible for all the group's non-regulated or commercial activities. 'And you must have the intellect to become a technical expert with a bit of quick study if you need to. But it's not very productive for a CFO to try to solve everything themselves.'

For example, if a new accounting treatment will affect the presentation of the accounts and how investors see the company's results, the CFO will want to know what questions investors and other external stakeholders are likely to ask and how to respond to those questions. The CFO will also want to know about any relevant information that he or she might need to highlight to users of accounts.

'The CFO needs to be able to differentiate what is commercially important or has a cash implication for the business from how the numbers are technically presented in order to comply with accounting standards,' says Longhurst. 'So I need my technical experts to focus on making sure that we're complying with our disclosure requirements and I delve into the commercial substance – what are the implications or threats to the business? Then I have to articulate those to the board and the shareholders in order to help develop the strategic direction of the business.'

Longhurst says that a CFO needs to be able to take a step back from the detail and act as an objective 'fresh pair of eyes' instead. 'You want to take that detail, scan it, identify the obvious errors, omissions and questions, and feed back to the team. As a CFO, you're involved in so many different areas – you might have a couple of tax issues or an acquisition to oversee, as well as your basic compliance and management accounting work. So the only way you can keep on top of all that is by dipping in and out of these activities to keep them going in the right direction and put them back on track if they need corrective action.'

In addition to drawing on the expertise that exists within their team, CFOs or senior leaders in professional services also need to maintain their own technical knowledge by doing their continuing professional development (CPD) and reading around what is happening in both their own industry and the wider business world. Only then can they have a true understanding of how what they do fits into a broader context.

Technical knowledge is not enough

Yet, although it is undeniably important to have strong technical expertise, you're highly unlikely to make it to a senior finance leadership role on the basis of your technical expertise alone. You will probably need to possess a wide range of other skills and attributes and have benefited from, and learned from, a variety of professional experiences. Whether you regard that as good news or bad news will probably depend on your own personality, interests and skills.

'If you're assessing a range of accountants for future potential, and they all have some sort of professional qualification, what you will be looking for in addition to certain personal attributes is how proactive they've been in their jobs in terms of looking for extra work. Have they sought out projects and proactively approached their boss to say: "What else can I do? How can I grow?"' says Karen Young, director with UK-based recruitment expert Hays Senior Finance. 'And when you have a face-to-face meeting with them, you will be looking for a sense of natural curiosity that leads to them asking a question, listening to your response and offering insight back.'

She also singles out communication skills as being 'what can make the difference between someone being average and someone going to the top and being extremely successful'. Communication skills are particularly important given that finance leaders need to make sure they are understood by people who may not have the same level of financial expertise as they do.

'To be a successful finance person, it is essential to have very good people and communication skills,' says Geraldine Matchett, CFO of Dutch nutrition and material science giant Royal DSM. 'I always make sure I turn any financial concern into conversations that fit the people involved. It's very rare that I refer to technical terms or IFRS standards. Only with my finance teams do I ever get carried away and indulge in technical financial mumbo jumbo. And even with them, the art is in translating the issue into what it really means for the business.'

Jack McGinnis, CFO of Fortune 500 company ManpowerGroup and a former partner at EY in the United States, concurs that communication skills are vital. 'Most partners in public accounting firms have very good relationship and communication skills,' he says. 'That's what allowed them to get to that level. Having technical knowledge or subject matter expertise on something like derivatives accounting gets you so far. But if you can't really communicate those concepts in plain English to business people, you'll have difficulty advancing to a higher role in client service going forward.'

Partner potential

As trusted advisers, audit and tax partners in professional services firms will be expected to demonstrate strong and up-to-date technical knowledge to ensure that the clients they work for comply with appropriate standards and regulation.

'Technical skills are a given,' says Rachel Campbell, global head of people, performance and culture at KPMG International. 'I don't think that you can compensate for lack of technical ability with great relationship skills, for example. You really need to be grounded in the technical aspects of what it means to be a good audit partner or tax partner.'

Having said that, if those partners go on to senior leadership roles within their firms, like CFOs they will be able to draw on the expertise of their teams and they will usually have access to other technical experts within their firm who have specialist knowledge of a certain area of accounting or tax.

Besides being technically able, a potential partner will need to be determined, hard-working and resilient, according to Campbell, as well as being someone who acts with integrity and is prepared to challenge. They will also have to be good at building relationships, curious and willing to ask questions. 'That's so fundamental to being a successful partner,' says Campbell. 'You spot those people and you cultivate them.'

Some finance professionals may fear that their socio-economic background may preclude them from ever making partner but Campbell says the notion that a career in finance is essentially the reserve of an elite group of people is changing. She points to the school-leaver programmes being launched in the UK by the big firms as an example of this and says that a lot is being done to open up the profession, in terms of both gender and other types of diversity.

'When I joined the profession, recruitment came from a handful of universities and often a handful of courses,' she says. 'Those days are behind us in terms of entry into the profession, but I think there is work to do to maintain the breadth and diversity of the talent in the firms at more senior levels.'

Need a niche?

There is some debate as to whether having a niche – for example in corporate finance, tax or treasury – is a help or a hindrance to finance professionals looking to advance in their careers.

On the one hand, many of the finance leaders who were interviewed for this book emphasized the importance of gaining a broad base of knowledge, ideally including some operational experience. That's because the more that a finance professional moves around between different functions and divisions, the broader the view of the organization that he or she will have and the greater the impact he or she will be able to make. Many finance professionals gain that knowledge by acting as the finance directors of an operating subsidiary or by working on cross-functional projects with colleagues in different departments across the organization.

Longhurst was in charge of treasury – alongside a host of other responsibilities – when he worked in Saudi Arabia as a finance manager for oil giant Shell. He found that having a wide remit helped to broaden out his expertise. 'Having one of those finance manager roles where you're running the whole shop in one part of the business is a great training ground,' he explains.

On the other hand, having a niche can be very useful in today's competitive environment, argues Jonathan Ng, executive director, qualification and education at the Hong Kong Institute of Certified Public Accountants (CPAs). 'It means you stand out from the crowd and it improves your employability. The financial market is very sophisticated these days and very diverse. You can't learn everything. So once you have the general skills, pick an area and become a specialist in that area.'

David Tilston, former CFO of Innovia Group, believes that if you work in a large organization, it may be a good idea to develop a niche early on in your career 'so that you are noticed as being good in one area and as someone who is worth developing'.

Certainly, niche proved to be an advantage for Lucinda Bell, finance director of British Land. She has a background in tax and she used her specialism in this area to enhance her reputation and build up a powerful external network. 'Through the work I did in developing the real estate investment trust (REIT) regime in the UK, I dealt with both the government and with very senior people from other property companies,' she says. 'But it was my specific skill set, together with my ability to make the complicated sound straightforward, that put me in the position where I got access to all those people in the first place.'

Nevertheless, she acknowledges that holding a role as head of tax is not the most common stepping stone to a CFO job. 'Often you would have been finance director of an operating subsidiary and sometimes you get treasurers – particularly in real estate – but there aren't so many of the tax people,' she says.

Life-long learning

If you want to progress to a senior level in finance – and even if you want to keep your current job – you need to be committed to developing yourself throughout your career. And that means taking your CPD seriously. 'Life-long learning is important,' says Ng. 'As someone progresses from a junior to senior role, their technical expertise will grow and they will need to make the most of their CPD. Accounting and auditing standards are not static – they change frequently and new regulation comes in. Also, there are advances in technology. All of these require finance professionals to stay up to date and improve their knowledge.'

While professional accountancy bodies require their members to do CPD, life-long learning extends beyond that. A finance professional who is committed to life-long learning will read industry publications and undertake courses that are offered by their professional bodies – the Hong Kong Institute of CPAs offers a development programme for financial controllers, for example, while the American Institute of Public Certified Accountants runs expert witness skills workshops for forensic accountants and webcasts on topics such as cyber security.

In the UK, the Institute of Chartered Accountants in England and Wales (ICAEW) offers a wide range of development opportunities for ambitious finance professionals. Among these is the Financial Talent Executive Network (F-TEN), which is a business leadership, mentoring and networking programme designed for aspiring CFOs. It is aimed at finance professionals who are one or two career stages away from a group CFO or equivalent-level role. Other development programmes run by ICAEW include the Developing Leadership in Practice programme, which aims to help finance professionals in practice develop and hone the leadership qualities expected of a new or aspiring partner, and the Network of Finance Leaders programme, which is designed for line managers and senior managers who want to move into a strategic leadership role.

Usually, there are also opportunities for professional development in the organization in which you work. 'Part of your professional development could be working in different business units or different finance roles, for example, doing an acquisition,' says Tilston. 'As you move through your career, it is important to take on different roles and build up your all-round experience.'

Campbell developed herself by acquiring broad client experience while she was working in KPMG's audit service line. 'I've always sought out taking on something new and different, whether that's within audit, or another part of the business, whether that's working overseas or within a different sector,' she says. 'When I meet new graduates who have their career mapped out, I always tell them to give that up because if you chase a role you will never get there. The best thing you can do is to constantly challenge yourself with new and different things. Then your career will take care of itself.'

Reflecting on how she's approached learning during her career, Campbell says: 'Partly it's because of my curious nature, but I was always keen to try new things. I was quite happy to be out of my comfort zone and take lateral moves – not necessarily upward moves – just to build up my experiences. I believe it really works. I look at my job now and I regularly reference different, challenging times in my career and go back to those when I'm thinking about how to approach something.'

One way that would-be CFOs can expand their skill sets is by studying for treasury qualifications and/or doing a stint in treasury so that they learn about cash and liquidity management, derivatives and funding, among other topics. In comparison with financial reporting, which has a tendency to be backward looking and focused on controls and processes, treasury is both dynamic and forward looking. It entails managing the organization's cash on a day-to-day basis, negotiating with banks, ensuring there is enough liquidity to keep the business going, raising finance to pay for upcoming acquisitions and managing the organization's foreign exchange risks.

David Tilston credits his treasury qualification – the MCT from the Association of Corporate Treasurers – with helping him significantly in his career. 'With the MCT qualification, you take exams based on typical, real-life situations, where there is not necessarily a right or a wrong answer. What I got from that is an extremely good toolbox of techniques and skills plus experience in the classroom of dealing with ambiguity and complex situations.'

Contact with the board

A finance professional who is rising fast in an organization will, at some point, probably be called on to present to the board (and possibly other parties besides, such as external investors). The prospect of presenting to the most senior group of people within the company will inevitably be daunting, but it is also a great opportunity to learn a skill that will be invaluable in the future. With the right preparation, it is not something that should be feared.

'Your CFO should be able to advise you on what to expect and which issues are likely to come up,' explains Tilston. 'They will know where some of the board members are coming from and what they are particularly focused on. If there is a particularly contentious issue, rather than waiting for it to come up, it's probably better to pre-empt it in the presentation and say: "Fundamentally, you've got two options. I don't know which of the two options the board feels most comfortable pursuing but these are the two options that you should consider." This helps to frame the board debate if a board debate is required.'

Tilston also advises finance professionals to be clear and concise when presenting to the board and to bear in mind that not all the board members will have a financial background. 'Boards get given a lot of information so keep the points to a minimum around the key areas,' he says. 'Focus on the most important points and don't get lost in the detail. Board members may well want to drill down into the key points, in which case you will need the background information. But make it very simple for them to understand the issues and come to a decision. Also, make sure you prepare for the worst questions that you would not want to be asked and decide how you would handle them if they came up.' Prior to the board meeting, it is also a good idea to hold a run-through of your presentation in front of the CFO and other members of your team. That way you can get feedback on how you have made your points and practise answering questions related to the content of your presentation.

Should you study for an MBA?

Some ambitious finance professionals choose to study for a Master of Business Administration (MBA) as part of their career development. There are a number of valid reasons for this. First, an MBA will give them a broader perspective of the business world, since MBA courses tend to cover topics such as entrepreneurship, leadership, management, marketing, strategy and technology in addition to finance. As they are known to be academically challenging and a big time commitment on top of a day job, gaining an MBA can be a great way of enhancing your CV and setting you apart from your peers. Having an MBA can also be a big boost to your salary since certain employers will pay a premium to recruit an MBA graduate. Research by Fortune in 2015 found that the expected median starting salary for recent MBA graduates in the United States that year was $100,000, an advantage of $45,000 over what employers were paying for graduates with bachelor's degrees.[1]

The answer to the question of whether an MBA will help a finance professional to rise to the top in his or her career varies according to the market. So in the United States, the MBA is seen as the traditional route into investment banking, but CPAs may also choose to study for an MBA because they see it as a broader business training that complements the technical expertise they acquired when they were studying for their CPA. Furthermore, many individuals make it to CFO without gaining an accountancy qualification at all. Around half of CFOs in the Fortune 500 have an MBA, compared with 40 per cent who are qualified accountants.[2]

While MBAs are a popular choice for aspiring finance leaders in the United States, a combination of a CPA and good work experience can be an equally effective means of taking your career to the next level, as Jack McGinnis proves. Now CFO of recruitment giant ManpowerGroup, McGinnis earned his CPA very early on while he was working in practice at EY. He then debated studying for an MBA while he was working his way up the ranks at the firm. 'I went to one of the senior partners and asked him whether he thought I needed an MBA,' he recalls. 'His advice to me was this: "You can certainly go and get one, but it's a big commitment so you'll have to devote a lot of time to it. My advice to you is take all the time that you would put into an MBA and put it into your job here. Then you will make partner faster and it won't matter if you have an MBA." Looking back, I think he was right.'

MBAs are also popular in Hong Kong, which is a steady supplier of finance professionals to the mighty Chinese economy. Many accountants who qualified as CPAs in Hong Kong go on to study for MBAs as they believe the master's degree will enhance their entrepreneurial qualities, according to Ng. 'Many of the people who do MBAs are thinking of starting their own business,' he says. 'An MBA puts a lot of emphasis on the global perspective and best practice.'

In other markets, such as Australia, Canada, New Zealand, South Africa and the UK, the chartered accountancy training is considered to be a good grounding in business rather than just finance. Therefore, accountants who trained in these countries are less likely to feel that they need an MBA to further their careers. 'There is a pretty much globally accepted view that the Australian, Canadian, New Zealand, South African and UK qualifications are the equivalent of the CPA/MBA combination in the US in the sense they confer the strongest mix of technical and commercial capability,' explains Freebairn.

What's more, there is less willingness in these markets to accept an MBA as an alternative to a professional accountancy qualification. 'If someone has an MBA, but they don't have an accountancy qualification, they will be very good on a wide range of business matters,' says Longhurst. 'In some cases, however, they may not feel that confident with the financial details, which is crucial if you are to be a CFO.'

International experience

Over a third of the finance directors who were surveyed for Hays' 2013 Report *DNA of an FD* had worked outside the UK at some point during their career. Of those who had worked abroad, most had worked in Europe (56 per cent), followed by North America (28 per cent) and Africa (20 per cent). An overwhelming majority of finance directors who had completed an overseas stint (93 per cent) said that the experience had definitely aided their career advancement.

If you are developing your career in a multinational company, you are more likely to need international experience to progress your career than if you are working for a domestic company. Nevertheless, the rapid pace of globalization means that international experience is becoming increasingly relevant to all finance professionals.

'We are living in a very connected world,' says Ng. 'If a finance professional in Hong Kong has a job in a multinational company, they must be prepared to be mobile and to oversee operations, not just in Asia-Pacific but further afield.' Fortunately, he says, the international transferability of accountancy qualifications enables finance professionals to practise in locations outside their home market.

For example, cross-border activities and transactions take place between China and Hong Kong. Hence Hong Kong finance professionals are expected to be able to work in both places. 'An individual has to be familiar with the culture in both China and Hong Kong,' explains Ng. 'I know people who are in internal audit or in the finance departments of companies and they are travelling a lot because they need to oversee operations in different offices in Asia-Pacific. It's quite common nowadays.'

While finance skills and qualifications are transferrable, and many multinationals do move their finance people around the world, it is not necessarily straightforward for a finance professional to take a job in a company that is based in a different jurisdiction from his or her own due to the differences in accounting standards that are applied. So a finance professional who is familiar with the principles-based International Financial Reporting Standards used in the UK may not be considered suitable for a job with a US company that applies rule-based-US GAAP to its financial standards. This difficulty can be overcome if sector experience is deemed more important than knowledge of the standards, however.

Ultimately, it's hard to dispute the value of international experience. 'I would say that international experience is a must,' says Julie Brown, CFO of FTSE 100 medical equipment manufacturer Smith & Nephew. 'The world is increasingly mobile, open and transparent and most large companies compete on a global scale.

'I went from Britain, to Portugal, to Latin America, where I dealt with countries such as Argentina, Brazil, Chile, Colombia, Ecuador, Mexico and Venezuela. Then I came back to London and now I have a very broad role. I frequently deal with China, Latin America and other emerging markets. So it's really valuable to have been in those types of countries and to have seen how they work. It gives you such a good insight into what it takes to do business in different parts of the world, with people who have different types of skill sets. It also gives you the ability to get the best out of teams. You learn to recognise strengths and also to recognise where you've got a few weaknesses. It's really important to get the best out of diverse teams in a multinational environment.'

ABC – a lesson in being the best

Julie Brown, now CFO of Smith & Nephew, was given some valuable advice on how to succeed in finance early in her career – by the then CFO of chemicals giant ICI.

'He talked about the ABC of success, which I believe in and which I refer to when I'm talking to groups,' she recalls. 'The "A" stands for ability – your own ability to learn so that you're knowledgeable in your area of responsibility. The "B" stands for bravery – being willing to take opportunities when they present themselves and willing to take the risks associated with those opportunities. The "C" stands for chance – senior positions are often about being in the right place, at the right time, and seizing the opportunity.'

Brown believes her own career journey demonstrates the ABC of success. She started out by qualifying as both a chartered accountant and a chartered tax adviser with KPMG. Then she got her first glimpse of what life would be like in industry when KPMG sent her on secondment to act as an interim finance director for one of its clients. She led a reasonably large team that improved the organization's financial controls and segregation of duties as well as the forecasts and other financial information that went to the management team. As a result, the management team and the finance team could work together more effectively on improving the business.

'The experience gave me a taste of the value that you can add when you work in industry,' says Brown. 'That's not to say that you can't add value when you're working in one of the larger professional firms, because I think you can, but the value you can add is different. When you're working as a finance director or CFO, compared with working as an adviser, you have complete accountability for the success or failure of that company. You live or die by the results as a consequence.'

Although she was offered the opportunity to stay on with KPMG's client in a permanent position, Brown decided that if she wanted to pursue a career in industry she would be better off joining the largest multinational company in the UK at that time, which was ICI.

'The idea was that I would join ICI and be a very small cog in a very large wheel for about two years to learn about blue-chip multinational practices,' says Brown. 'I thought that way I could add a great deal more value to a lot of companies.'

As it happened, though, Brown effectively ended up staying with the company for twenty-five years because ICI demerged its pharmaceutical bioscience businesses into a new company called Zeneca, which then merged with rival Astra AB to become AstraZeneca. By the time she left AstraZeneca to join Smith & Nephew in 2013, Brown had served a stint as the company's interim CFO during a period of transition for the management team.

'I never had a plan to become a FTSE CFO,' says Brown. 'I was motivated to join industry at the beginning because industry was so much more exciting than auditing and I thought you could add real value. My plan was to broaden my experience base and learn from the best, which at that stage was ICI.'

Brown joined ICI as the finance head for research and development, but the company's impressive talent management programmes resulted in her holding eleven different roles, in four different countries, over the course of twenty-five years. During this time, she had both finance and general management responsibilities including being vice president of corporate strategy and research, marketing company president of AstraZeneca Portugal and regional vice president of Latin America. She puts the breadth of experience she gained down to her managers being prepared to take risks on her as well as her being prepared to take risks and seize the opportunities that came with them.

'My drive to be the best that I could be in whichever part of the organisation I was working in was really powerful,' she says. So when she was country head of Portugal, her team increased the company's market share so that it rose from sixth place to second place in the ranking of pharmaceutical companies. When she was in Latin America, she oversaw double-digit growth in sales and profit growth of more than 30 per cent each year. 'It was that kind of drive,' she says. 'But it was also the power of working with teams – extremely diverse teams – to deliver great results for the organisation.'

Brown credits her line managers with having given her the opportunities that she needed to succeed. 'They gave me considerable bandwidth and enlarged my remit, sometimes encouraging me to go far further than even I thought I was capable of. I think they were testing me to see how far I could go and I've always really appreciated that. Undoubtedly one of the reasons I am where I am today is because people I've worked for really gave me an opportunity to shine and grow.'

Additionally, having two major commercial roles as well as the head of strategy role under her belt helped to set Brown apart from other professionals 'who had only gone down the finance route'. She believes that these roles have been crucial in making her a more effective CFO.

'When you've led a business yourself, you know the additional complexities of leading a business,' she says. 'When you're in that seat, managing your own P&L, having everybody dependent on you for their jobs, you know that if the sales line doesn't deliver, you're going to have to restructure the cost base. You feel an incredible sense of responsibility towards the people in the organisation. Having had those experiences makes you a better CFO and helps you to partner with the CEO on a much better footing.'

The skills of a CFO

Today's CFOs typically have a very broad range of responsibilities that fall into four main categories: oversight of the financial reporting process and financial management activities (including accounting, insurance, risk management, tax and treasury); operational leadership of the finance function and any other functions that may report into them such as HR, investor relations, legal, IT and procurement; commercial and strategic partnership with the business; and management of relationships with external stakeholders including analysts, investors, lenders and the media.

Put another way, EY's 2016 report, *The DNA of the CFO*,[3] defines the responsibilities of CFOs in six key areas: ensuring business decisions are grounded in sound financial criteria; providing insight and analysis to support the CEO and other senior managers; leading key initiatives in finance that support overall strategic goals; funding, enabling and executing strategy set by the CEO; developing and defining the overall strategy for the organization; and representing the organization's progress on strategic goals to external stakeholders.

In practice, what this means is that the CFO is using financial information to help the CEO to make important decisions about which business areas and markets to invest in; leading finance projects that support that decision-making process – for example, scenario planning of what an investment might return in different circumstances; raising money to fund the investment; working with the CEO to set strategy; and being able to report on how the organization is delivering on its strategy to analysts, investors and other stakeholders.

Given the breadth of responsibilities that CFOs have, it is not surprising that EY's report also highlighted the pressures that they are under. Over half (52 per cent) said they cannot focus on strategic priorities by delegating responsibilities because of a lack of necessary skills in the finance team. A similar amount (51 per cent) cannot focus on strategic priorities because of increasing operational responsibilities while 56 per cent cannot focus on strategic priorities because of time spent on compliance, controls and costs.

These different responsibilities are reflected in the skills that a CFO needs to do his or her job. So Hays' research, *DNA of an FD*,[4] found that over a third (36 per cent) of finance directors thought that commercial understanding is the most important skill for a finance director to possess, followed by people management (18 per cent) and strategic planning (14 per cent).

'A CFO should be able to talk and act strategically,' says Ng. 'When you take up a senior position, you need to be able to steer the team and company towards the goal and results. And you are expected to drive change, manage people, focus on results and add value. It is not just about crunching the numbers.'

Ng also hones in on the need for a CFO to have the right mindset. 'You need to remind yourself that you are a service provider,' he says. 'So you need to align what you do across departments to deliver a service to your customers. That mentality will drive excellence.'

'Having a broader span of responsibility means that the ability to hire and manage a team of experts in individual disciplines is more important today than it was 20 or 30 years ago,' says Tilston. 'The outward-facing aspects of the role are also more important than they were 20 or 30 years ago. At that time, two or three banks might lend your organisation all the money that it needed. Only the very largest listed companies issued bonds. Now smaller companies and private equity-owned companies are issuing bonds that are publicly traded in the high-yield markets or else they are arranging private placements of debt. These developments have brought a new set of external stakeholders, such as institutional investors, that most CFOs and finance directors would not have needed to deal with in the past. In addition, risk management is much more important than it was 20 or 30 years ago as a result of the greater focus on good corporate governance.'

Being able to manage relationships with investors – whether those are institutional, private equity or retail investors or even family shareholders in the case of a privately owned business – is a crucial skill for CFOs and they will always need to have an accurate and convincing answer to the compelling question: How is the company doing? They will only be able to provide that answer if they oversee a solid and reliable finance function that can produce forecasts and results quickly and accurately. In a private equity environment, CFOs will be particularly judged on their cash management and cash forecasting since private equity investors tend to be highly focused on cash.

The CFOs of multinational companies operate at a global level, so they need to be confident managing cross-cultural teams and maintaining relationships with investors and lenders in different regions and time zones. 'You have to be adept at communication with a range of cultures,' says Tilston. 'Sometimes the time zone difference may mean you communicate primarily by email and then you get into the danger of people misunderstanding what you're saying. To understand other cultures, it's important to visit your company's operations in different countries.'

Bell also emphasizes the importance of relationship skills, highlighting that these are crucial to ensuring that the CFO can get through discussions on difficult topics and still go on to have 'close, connected' relationships with colleagues and external stakeholders. In addition, she highlights the importance of CFOs having emotional resilience. 'You have to be prepared to say things other people may not want to hear,' she explains. 'And you have to be prepared to argue your position, possibly at a moment's notice. Emotional resilience is important because you have to be able to do that and be very clear about what is the right thing for the company from your perspective.'

Finally, it appears that there is no escaping good, old-fashioned hard work when it comes to making it to the top – no matter how skilled and capable you are. According to *DNA of an FD*, three-quarters (75 per cent) of the finance directors surveyed said that being hard-working had aided their career success.

IT and systems

Many CFOs are put in charge of the IT function even if they have no technological background whatsoever. This is because IT systems tend to be expensive to implement and maintain, so it seems sensible for someone with a good grip on costs to be in charge of them. Even when CFOs don't directly oversee the IT function, perhaps because a chief technology officer holds that role, they will still need to work closely with the IT department because they will have IT systems for finance and they will also be involved in approving the costs for new IT systems within the organization. 'You've got to roll up your sleeves and try to get stuck in and understand it,' is how Tilston sums it up. 'But you're unlikely to be an expert.'

Having responsibility for IT is not something that CFOs necessarily get excited about because it can be a heavy burden. Technology is changing fast, which makes keeping up with it a challenge for people who do have a technological background, let alone those who don't. And those who sign off a seven-figure spend on a system that collapses on the second day after 'go-live', resulting in organizational chaos and a massive loss of data, will usually find themselves looking for a new job soon afterwards.

For this reason, it is helpful for would-be CFOs to have had some exposure to IT and systems as part of their career development – perhaps by being part of a cross-functional team in charge of rolling out new software across an organization. This will help them to understand not only the technological issues that can arise, but also the impact of the changes on the people and processes within the organization. An IT implementation is rarely just an IT implementation; it usually entails a widespread training programme and an overhaul of people's working practices as well. It may lead to redundancies, which could mean there is significant resistance to the new platform within the organization.

Anyone who wants to become a CFO cannot be frightened of IT. CFOs are continually involved in the management of change within their organization and IT is a fundamental part of change. Fortunately, there are ways in which CFOs can manage IT effectively. 'Firstly, you recruit the best IT people that you can,' says Tilston, although he acknowledges that this can be difficult when you're not an expert yourself. 'Secondly, use good, reliable, external IT consultants if you are looking to do anything significant.'

The technical route to CFO: Geraldine Matchett's story

Geraldine Matchett is a true European citizen. Half-British, half-Swiss – she grew up in France and completed her tertiary education in England, doing an undergraduate degree in geography at the University of Reading, followed by a master's degree in sustainable development at the University of Cambridge.

After leaving Cambridge, Matchett worked for UK utility company Thames Water for a couple of years before deciding that she wanted to gain an additional qualification. 'When I was at Thames Water I looked around and realised that most people who had interesting jobs had a professional qualification,' she says. 'I also noticed that the finance team was involved in everything, so given that I'm curious and I like to be involved in all aspects of a company, I opted for the chartered account-ancy route rather than a master's degree in environmental law.'

So Matchett joined KPMG in London and soon found herself assigned to the audit of Swiss confectionary giant Nestlé. After four years, she moved to Deloitte in Switzerland to head up the global audit of testing, inspec-tion and certification multinational SGS, which is headquartered in Geneva. While she was there, she came to the attention of the then CEO of SGS, Sergio Marchionne, who offered her a job. At the time, the rules didn't require a cooling-off period, so she was able to switch to SGS easily, initially in a corporate finance role.

Three months after Matchett's arrival, SGS's group financial controller left the business and she was promoted into the role. 'I jumped right in at the deep end,' she recalls. 'When I became group controller, I was thirty-two. I was the youngest ever group controller for a company that was more than 100 years old and employed over 85,000 people across 140 countries. I was also the first woman to ever be SGS's group controller.'

In many companies, the group controller role is a great role to have, says Matchett. 'You are in charge of all the financial reporting and analysis upwards from an internal perspective and outwards in terms of information provided to the financial markets. You also get heavily involved in the management reporting, looking at how businesses can improve their performance. Usually you end up getting very involved in efficiency, cost optimisation and restructuring programmes. And you are at the crossroads of just about everything. Setting targets requires knowing the company extremely well.'

The group controller role can also be a great way for an enthusiastic finance professional to raise their profile within the organization. 'You're in that interesting space where you're very connected with all parts of the organisation so you know what is going on, while, at the same time, you're in daily contact with the management board, executive committee and supervisory board. You're working closely with investor relations and you work with the auditor so you can keep up to date in terms of your technical knowledge as well. It's a very demanding but quite a fascinating role.'

It is also – in Matchett's view – the best possible preparation for being the CFO. 'After a while, when you see the numbers, you are able to have an opinion about them because you know exactly where they come from,' she explains. 'You are able to judge whether you believe them, whether they "look normal" or whether something is strange. That is not something a book is going to teach you. It comes with time – from interacting with all parts of the company and turning figures into insights.'

When it comes to interpreting the financial information, there will be 'some people of whom you need to ask ten different questions, while of others you will only need to ask one', says Matchett. So she believes that the skill that a group controller learns is to know who is a 'ten-question' person and who is a 'one-question' person. This is a particularly crucial skill in a multinational company where some subsidiaries will be more willing than others to disclose the real story behind their figures.

After she had served as SGS's group financial controller for six years, the company's CFO left and Matchett was offered his job. 'It depends what you're expecting,' was her cautious response to the job offer. 'If you want a big wheeler-dealer, M&A-driven CFO, then don't pick me because I don't have an investment banking background. If, however, you want a CFO who knows the business and is connected with the organisation, and who can understand and work with everyone in the organisation, then I am very interested!'

Matchett was just thirty-eight when she was appointed CFO of SGS in 2010, becoming both the youngest CFO and the only female CFO in the SIX Swiss Exchange SMI index, which is the index of large-cap quoted companies in Switzerland. But she quickly established a reputation for herself as a respected finance leader. In 2014, she was voted CFO of the Year for large companies in Switzerland by the CFO Forum Switzerland. That same year, she was headhunted for the CFO role at Royal DSM, where she is also a member of the management board and oversees the group's operations in Africa alongside her finance responsibilities.

Looking back on her career, Matchett believes that her ability to connect with others is a fundamental reason for her success. 'At the end of the day, a finance person can only bring value if he or she can translate our technical training into meaningful business insights,' she says. 'Of course it is important to be strong technically, because others will take the fact you know what you are talking about for granted, but it is by no means enough on its own. The way you make a difference is by making your knowledge relevant and accessible to everyone around you, from colleagues to investors.'

She adds: 'In addition, you can only be a good controller or CFO if you know what's going on in the company. And people will only tell you what's really going on if you are able to make yourself very approachable. They need to know that if they have bad news, you will be supportive and willing to help find solutions.'

The skills of a partner

Individuals who become senior leaders in professional services firms tend to share the same skills and capabilities as CFOs. So they have commercial nous, problem-solving skills and an ability to think strategically. They also possess the excellent communication and people skills that are necessary to succeed in the fiercely competitive, matrix organizational structures of professional services firms.

The need for these skills is emphasized by a 2014 report by recruiter Hays, entitled *DNA of a Partner*,[5] which found that 59 per cent of partners placed being commercially aware in their top three tips for the next generation of partners. Furthermore, 40 per cent advised the next generation to develop their people skills, 32 per cent said they should get involved with the business and not just the numbers and 26 per cent recommended that aspiring partners develop their advisory skills.

Unlike the finance function of a company, where the leadership model is based on a hierarchy reaching all the way up to the CFO, the client obligations of partners within professional services firms mean that they need to be able to influence and engage people in different service lines, in different countries, in different regions – people who may not have even heard of them, let alone report to them. Senior leaders in professional services also need to be mindful of the fact that the other partners in the business are effectively 'co-owners' of the business, so they need to get their buy-in to strategic decisions; they can't just roll out policy decisions in the way that a company management team can.

'Success in practice initially relies on a finance professional having the right technical experience,' says Sharron Gunn, executive director, members, commercial & shared services at ICAEW. 'But a successful partner brings in new business, sells to people, makes decisions, and manages and motivates staff. So it's a whole different skill set from the technical skill set they developed as they moved up the ranks.'

Besides their technical expertise, the people who rise to the top of the large professional services firms usually have outstanding client-facing skills that they have honed from working on client engagements over the years. They make it their business to learn about their client's business and to ask the kinds of questions that will enable them to understand their clients' business problems and come up with potential solutions (for which they can then charge fees to implement). These solutions might either be direct opportunities for them and their team or opportunities that they can provide to other professionals within the firm. While their role is to drive revenues, they won't necessarily describe themselves as sales people per se because they appreciate that that can be off-putting to clients.

'I never did any what you call traditional sales training,' says Sacha Romanovitch, CEO of Grant Thornton UK. 'Everything I've done has always been around: "How can I understand the context of this situation, what's needed to add value?" Then I worked with others to help create the solution. I have an anathema to the word "sales" in professional services because I think everything you do should be about creating value for people. If anybody is out selling a product, then there's something not quite right.'

She continues: 'If you really understand what's valuable to a client in the long term, you will sometimes say: "You don't need this." If you're focused on sales, I don't think you'll always do that.'

McGinnis worked his way up to become partner at EY before leaving to move into industry. He specialized in audit for financial services businesses in the days before independence rules prohibited auditors offering certain types of advisory services. 'On large accounts I would also perform consulting services, such as process reviews to improve reconciliations,' he says. 'I wasn't trained in sales skills, because if you were good at client service, sales came naturally since the client valued your work and capabilities and often requested additional services.

'Once you had established a deep relationship with a client, they trusted that you were bringing good ideas to them and so the door was opened. If you were good with communication and relationships, this happened very naturally. Those same skills meant you were placed on the largest accounts early in your career and allowed to work with others with similar traits as you progressed. Ultimately, client service is critical. If you are an outstanding client service partner, you will have plenty of other opportunities within the firm.'

Julie Teigland, regional managing partner for Germany, Switzerland and Austria at EY, learned to sell audits by working with a retired banker who was contracted to EY. Soon she had done so many client meetings in the Munich and Düsseldorf areas that she had become really good at them. 'Once you do enough sales calls, you have no fear anymore,' she says. 'You lose your fear. The worst thing that's going to happen is someone is going to say "No" to you. But once I had done them over and over again, some were saying "Yes". So I knew I could win if I could get out there and do it.'

The secret to selling is simple, Teigland says. 'It is just a matter of listening to what people want and need and making sure that we are delivering exactly this. It is also about being authentic. I don't even consider it to be selling. I think it's actually part of my job to advise our clients on what and when certain things are needed.'

Teigland believes that a partner primarily needs to take a commercial view and know when to bring in the technical experts, if he or she is not a technical expert. 'Being able to see eye-to-eye with a CFO, that's something a technical expert can't always do,' she says. 'If you want to be a successful engagement partner on audit clients, you need to be able to do that yourself.'

Becoming a partner in a firm requires a finance professional to change his or her mindset, notes Lydia Lamdin, ICAEW's head of professional development. This is because a partner is a co-owner in a business, which means he or she has to take the same risks that the owners of businesses in other sectors take. 'The biggest challenge in practice, which people in business don't have in the same way, is that once you get to that top level, you might have a year where you take half your salary if the firm's really struggling. So a big part of the partner development work we do is about how people can shift their mind-sets from thinking like an employee to being an owner of an organisation.'

Career in audit

Audit might be much maligned but it is still a great preparation for a leadership role in professional services. 'There's no doubt that audit is a great springboard to do multiple things,' says Campbell. 'Although I'm in a different role now, when I became an audit partner it never actually crossed my mind not to stay with audit. I've always found it really rewarding and a good grounding for building business understanding and relationship skills. I would like everyone to come through audit in our firm.'

She continues: 'What I love about audit is that you get a level of access to a company that is very hard to get if you are a tax or an advisory partner.

You're licensed to convene the senior people in the firm that you're auditing, to go and meet with them, to spend time with them and to really understand what's going on.'

Campbell says that having the opportunity to interact with C-suite executives – an opportunity that comes with audit – has motivated her and made her a better professional overall. 'I love that side of the role,' she says. 'You can really wander the corridors and you have access to do so because to do a good audit, you have to really, deeply understand the business that you are auditing and know what makes that business tick. Also, I'm really comfortable that what we do is important in terms of building public trust and confidence.'

Chapter end

What are the key takeaways from this chapter?

- Professional expertise will probably be the bedrock of your success, whether you pursue a career in practice or in industry.
- If you want to become a CFO, doing a stint as group financial controller or holding another technical role will stand you in very good stead.
- Technical expertise alone is not enough to make you extremely successful. You also need to have good communication and relationship skills.
- A career in audit can be great preparation for a leadership role in professional services.
- To succeed in finance, you need to be committed to developing yourself – both through formal education and by building up your experience base.

Chapter 3

Career management

The secret to my success

'It's either resourcefulness or diligence. I do think that in the CFO job you have to have quite a degree of diligence to make it all the way to the top.'

Lucinda Bell, CFO, British Land

The secret to my success

'I always try to have a very open and approachable style and I think that has helped me tremendously. Even when I was coming up through public accounting as a manager, I was very approachable to my staff. It was much more productive because they didn't get hung up about asking questions and things got done.

'This attribute also helps you to have a really strong working relationship with senior management because they view you as someone they can get a straight answer from. They like interacting with you because of your open style.'

Jack McGinnis, CFO, ManpowerGroup

Do you need to be a qualified accountant to get to the top in finance? The answer to that question is clearly no – some of the people who were interviewed for this book are not qualified accountants – but it certainly helps a lot. Due to the level of financial complexity that exists within large organizations, a professional accountancy qualification is still regarded as the ideal start for anyone who wants to be a CFO one day. Alternatively, if you hope to make partner in the audit or tax service line of a large professional services firm, a qualification is absolutely essential.

'You don't need to have an accountancy qualification to be a CFO,' says Stephen Billingham, the former finance director of British Energy, which was once a constituent of the FTSE 100 index. 'But I think you do need a financial background, either from being a banker or from coming through the treasury route. Accounting is a very powerful qualification, however. If I started again, I would probably go down that route because it puts you in the running for the mainstream roles. Also, not having an accountancy qualification can make life harder because people query whether you have got the skills to do the job.'

Billingham himself took on a financial controller's job while he was at engineering consultancy WS Atkins in order to prove that he had those skills. 'It shows that you can take financial control of an organisation, be involved in preparing the annual report and the investor presentations, and manage a team of financial accountants that produce the report and presentations,' he explains.

In the UK, not only is it very common for the CFO to hold an accountancy qualification, the CEO is quite likely to have one as well. According to the 2016 FTSE 100 CEO Tracker[1] by recruiter Robert Half, almost one in four company bosses holds a chartered accountancy qualification with 55 per cent having a finance background.

In comparison, the situation is less clear-cut in the United States where the CPA has a formidable rival in the form of the MBA. There it is perfectly normal for a CFO – who may well be regarded as a business partner and a strategist, rather than a number cruncher – to lack a formal finance-related qualification altogether. 'Generally speaking, it's fairly common for CFOs to have a CPA or an MBA,' observes Jack McGinnis, CFO of ManpowerGroup. 'But it's not a requirement. There are people who have become finance experts as they rose in the business. They have devoted enough time to become subject matter experts in the areas that matter and have made up for not having an accountancy qualification that way.'

The apparently lower level of demand for CFOs with technical financial expertise in the United States has been influenced by the marked trend towards companies hiring chief accounting officers in the wake of the 2002 Sarbanes-Oxley Act. The stringent requirements of the act, particularly its requirements with regard to disclosures and internal controls, led to companies strengthening their accounting functions with the appointment of highly technical chief accounting officers who usually have a CPA qualification. This has effectively freed up US CFOs to be more strategic.

According to 2016 research by US executive search firm Russell Reynolds, the number of CFOs hired in the prior three years with corporate accounting/control experience had decreased to 38 per cent, compared with 51 per cent of CFOs appointed more than three years previously. Meanwhile, there was a growing trend for CFOs to have investment banking experience – 24 per cent of CFOs appointed in the previous three years had investment banking experience, compared with 17 per cent of those hired before then.[2]

The growth of the chief accounting officer role has essentially enabled CFOs in the United States to spend less time on accounting and more time working with the CEO to grow the business. They can also focus more on managing relationships with investors and other external stakeholders – something that is increasingly important in an age of activist shareholders.

An accountancy qualification is never going to be a disadvantage to you as you pursue your career in finance. But regardless of whether you already have an accountancy qualification, are studying for one, intend to study for one, or don't have one and don't plan to get one, you do need to put some time into planning your career if you want to get as far as your abilities will permit you.

What you do in the first ten years of your career, in particular, is really important, according to Billingham. 'The variety of experience that you get in the first ten years shows your potential. And the organisations that you work for are more important than your job title. Being called "director" early on does not necessarily help you over the course of your career. What actually helps you is what you have done.'

While many of the finance leaders who were interviewed for this book said they had never had a plan to become a CFO or senior partner in their firm, they managed their career in a way that set them up for long-term success. Regardless of how high you want to go in your own career, you can still learn from their stories.

Moving from practice to industry

If you have qualified as an accountant with a professional services firm and you don't want to pursue a career in practice, the question you are most likely to want to ask is this: When should I move from practice to industry?

This question is one that recruiters frequently encounter and there is no straightforward answer because it depends on a person's individual circumstances. It also depends on the economic environment at the time. During a time of economic stress, when job cuts are being made, there are often fewer roles available in industry. So it can make sense to stay in practice rather than rushing into an unsuitable role working for a company. On the other hand, a boom period might present lots of exciting opportunities in industry, with opportunities to progress that can't be matched in practice.

'Don't panic immediately after you have qualified,' is the advice of Karen Young, director of Hays Senior Finance. 'I don't think spending some time in practice post qualification should ever be a hindrance to a good job in industry as long as you are focusing on developing your transferable skills.'

So even if you have long-term aspirations to work in industry, you shouldn't rush to leave your career in practice if you're still enjoying it and, in the process, acquiring new skills, building your network and gaining client-facing experience. You should have an independent development plan in place and you may also have the opportunity to do a secondment into industry while you're still working in practice.

On the other hand, if you are not enjoying your career in practice, and you are just delivering audit paper after audit paper, while being kept at arm's length from clients, you should assess the extent to which you are building up transferable skills and decide whether now is the right time to move into industry.

Although it is important not to rush into a career in industry when you have trained in practice without weighing up your options carefully, neither should you go to the other extreme and procrastinate for years and years. 'There is a point several years down the line where it does become more difficult to compete for jobs with those who already have industry experience,' says Young.

Newly qualified accountants and accountants with up to three years' experience post-qualification normally find it fairly easy to move into industry. Once you get beyond that, it becomes progressively more challenging, however. So individuals who reach senior manager or partner-designate in an accountancy firm and then decide that they want to move into industry can find making the switch difficult, especially if economic conditions are poor.

The reason for this is that there will be heightened competition for the available jobs in industry. People who are trying to move into them straight from practice will find that they are competing with finance professionals who may have up to fifteen years' industry experience. In that situation, a hiring CEO or MD is likely to see a finance professional with a background in industry as a safer bet because he or she is more likely to have experience of managing cash and risk, growing a company and keeping it afloat.

So while it is not impossible to move from practice to industry at a later point in your career, it will usually be harder than if you had attempted it earlier on. 'You really, really have to prepare for the interviews, prove those transferrable skills and be able to cite examples with your client group that are relevant and valuable to that organisation,' explains Young. 'And you've got to pick the jobs that you apply for carefully. So if you have dealt with a lot of fast-moving consumer goods (FMCG) clients in the past, then focus on applying for jobs in the FMCG sector. You will have relevant experience to bring to bear and so stand a better chance of getting a job. Apply for other jobs, too, but be realistic since it may be harder to land a job in a sector you have had no exposure to within your client portfolio.'

At the very highest levels, it is possible for audit firm partners to move into CFO roles within industry, but this has become harder due to stringent 'cooling off' requirements in many jurisdictions. These requirements typically prevent individuals who have served as members of an organization's audit team from joining that organization in a position where they would have influence over the financial statements (for example, as CFO or financial controller) for a period of one or two years.

It is also important to bear in mind that a move to industry is not necessarily going to bring an immediate end to your career frustrations. If you want to move into industry from an audit role in practice, the chances are that many of the roles that you will be considered for are internal audit roles. Depending on the organization that you join, you may be expected to stick out internal audit for eighteen to twenty-four months before you progress into a management role. On a positive note, however, even if you think you are sick of audit, you will find that doing an internal audit role gives you the opportunity to find out about your new organization in depth and to add some commercial value through the activities you do. There may also be the opportunity to travel.

In addition to internal audit, many newly qualified accountants move into financial accountant roles within organizations. In these roles they will need to demonstrate technical expertise to ensure that the organization complies with its statutory obligations. People are less attracted to these roles, says Young, because they differ from the more 'glamorous' commercial accountant, management accountant and business partner roles that newly qualified accountants tend to envisage they will land when they first move into industry.

Young says: 'You show people the job specification and they say: "Oh, I'm going to do month end, I'm going to do reconciliations, I'm going to do the financial reporting for a specific deadline. And I'm going to be managing that process in the same way every month. It feels a lot like the routine in audit that I am trying to get away from." So when there are commercial accounting and management accounting jobs around for newly qualifieds, it can be hard to find people who say: "Yes, I really want that financial accountant job."'

While it may be more appealing for a newly qualified accountant to move into a commercial accounting or management accounting role that is focused on profit and loss (P&L), rather than a financial accountant or technical accountant role that is focused on the balance sheet, experience of a technical accounting role is sound preparation for being a CFO. 'It is important to have spent time in roles that look after the balance sheet so people know you can do technical jobs, as well as the more business-facing P&L jobs,' explains Young.

She also argues that it makes sense for ambitious finance professionals to take on this kind of role earlier rather than later in their careers. Otherwise, they may be in a position where they have attained a senior management job such as head of financial planning and analysis or head of management accounting, together with a substantial salary, and then have to think about taking a pay cut to apply for a hands-on, technical accounting job when their knowledge of statutory requirements may not be entirely up to date.

'If you are newly qualified and you don't get that technical, "managing the month-end process" under your belt, and you skip that to be a finance business partner in industry, it's going to be quite a tough gig to get to be CFO or finance director,' says Young. 'It's not impossible, but you are making the route harder. That's because if you've never done it yourself, you'll never be able to say "I managed the process and so I can manage other people doing it."'

Once a finance professional has moved from practice into industry, he or she needs to become alert to the fact that his or her new employer will not necessarily be as tuned in to developing him or her as their previous firm was. Professional services firms sell the skills of their people, so it is in their interests to develop them because that's what makes them money. The same argument doesn't necessarily hold in industry, where finance is often seen as a support function. 'People can get a real shock when they go into a big business,' says Lydia Lamdin, head of professional development at the Institute of Chartered Accountants in England and Wales. 'Their line manager may be too busy to actively support their development and the chances are there won't be structured career paths and development support already in place.'

Lamdin also identifies some other key differences between industry and practice. 'You don't get the same level of exposure to senior people in industry as you do in practice,' she says. 'And in practice, your job is about understanding what you need to do and having the confidence to do it. In industry, you've got to be very, very good at dealing with complexity and managing people – working out who you need to know, how you can get to know them and how you influence your way up. The professional services firms tend to have a hierarchical structure whereas most businesses work to a matrix structure.'

Relationship with your boss

The interviews conducted for this book suggest that the greatest determinants of your career success are likely to be your line managers. This is potentially worrying given that the number one reason why most people depart from their organization is that they don't like their boss – a Gallup poll in 2015 found that half of the US adults surveyed had left their job to get away from their manager.[3]

Furthermore, a bad relationship with a line manager does not affect only people on the lower rungs of the career ladder. One of the most common reasons why CFOs start looking for a new job is that a new CEO has come into their organization and the pair of them just don't see eye to eye.

Since your relationship with your boss can make or break your success at whichever career level you are at, it is in your interests to make sure that the relationship is as constructive as possible. Unfortunately, however, the likelihood is that during the course of your career, you will have at least one manager that you just can't get on with. Given that they will be standing between you and your career progression, what can you do if you find yourself in this situation?

'You may be able to improve the relationship over time so try to be constructive wherever possible,' says Young. 'Look at the reasons why the relationship is not working and try to address them. Is it because you are not getting a one-to-one meeting every month? Is your line manager not giving you enough support or giving you too much support? Try to work out what the issues are, put some fixes in and avoid getting personal.'

If that doesn't work, Young argues that you can walk away knowing you've put your best effort into trying to repair the relationship. She says: 'You can have an interview somewhere else and say: "They were micro-managing me. I professionally addressed that. They agreed and said they would stop, but I think it's their natural style. So we agreed that it wasn't right for either of us and I decided to move on. I do like to work autonomously and you've just told me that your culture enables people to do that, so it sounds like we would be the perfect partnership!"'

Young believes that if it is necessary you can admit that you've had issues with a direct line manager in a job interview. And in some situations it really will be necessary. For example, if you are a CFO who is looking to move organization after the arrival of a new CEO, the appointment of the new CEO will probably be public knowledge, so prospective employers will want to know why you want to move on so quickly after the CEO joined.

'It is acceptable if you broach it in the right way, be clear that it isn't personal and show what steps you've taken to address any challenges around communication styles or management needs,' she says. 'And you should be able to talk through it constructively, with a smile, at the interview.'

Working with HR functions, recruitment consultants and headhunters

Aside from your line managers, there are other groups of people who can have a very significant influence on your career. These are the internal HR functions of the organizations that you work for as well as external recruitment consultants and, as you progress to senior levels in your career, executive search firms (also known colloquially as 'headhunters'). The likelihood is that you will need to build strong relationships with all of these groups if you want to advance to your full potential.

'The first thing that anyone who is planning their career should think about is how they can use internal career development to get known to people who could potentially be sponsors of their job progression internally but also offer an opinion to head hunters even before head hunters make it onto your own radar,' advises Ronan Dunne, former CEO of Telefónica UK. 'In most organisations you build a reputation internally, then you get formal or informal sponsors as well as people who are slightly older and further on in their career who tend to be the first port of call for head hunters. It may not be a finance director who sponsors you. It may be the chief executive or managing director of one of the business units who perceives you as commercial and helpful. Head hunters don't just ring me about jobs that I might be suitable for, they ring me about people who are one or two levels down in the organisation.'

Having internal sponsorship can make a big difference to career progression, agrees Rachel Campbell, global head of people, performance and culture at KPMG International. 'It is absolutely the case that you need to have mentors but equally you need sponsors around you. One of my roles now is to look at up-and-coming talent and make sure they have both mentors and broad sponsorship. Nevertheless, to qualify for that support, they need to have the determination, skills and talent to take on the next big role.'

Regardless of whether a recruitment consultant makes contact when you are at a fairly junior level in your career, or a headhunter gets in touch later on, it is important that you take the opportunity to build a relationship with the person who has approached you, even if you don't find the job he or she is offering of interest at that time. 'Whenever I've been rung about a job, I've always made the effort to develop that relationship so that the person will always ring me back when they have a more interesting job, or else I can ring them when I have a job that needs filling,' says Dunne. 'You have to work on building relationships. So there has never been a head hunter's call that I have not returned, even if I have not been interested in that particular opportunity.'

Making sure that you have done your homework internally – and having a strong network of sponsors and people who are prepared to refer you – will stand you in good stead when you actually go out to meet headhunters, says Dunne. 'Then your reputation is built and when you articulate the role you have played in the business, you will be able to give them a story that they can cross-check because they will know other people who were involved in a particular business success.'

Smith & Nephew CFO Julie Brown discovered how headhunters monitor an individual's reputation when she stood down from the interim CFO job at AstraZeneca in 2012. The permanent CFO and her line manager, Simon Lowth, had been standing in as AstraZeneca's CEO while the board looked for a successor for David Brennan, the company's outgoing CEO. 'The FTSE 100 companies prefer to recruit people who have been in the CFO seat before,' explains Brown. 'So even if you just hold an interim CFO position in a FTSE 10 company, you immediately go onto the head hunters' radars. The day that we all returned to our previous roles, I had eleven calls from headhunters. Those led to me having the opportunity to become CFO at Smith & Nephew.'

Stephen Billingham, now a board chair, has been approached by headhunters about a steady stream of roles ever since he was group finance director of WS Atkins. Becoming a main board director put him on headhunters' radars and he has had both bad and good experiences of headhunters over the years. The bad experiences were when the headhunter in question knew little about his career history or expertise. The good experiences were when the headhunter presented a great opportunity to him – a case in point being when he was headhunted to join FTSE 100 company British Energy as group finance director.

'It was obvious to me that the head hunter had a job to shift,' recalls Billingham. 'But I didn't want to leave WS Atkins because I had just been through a successful turnaround. So it was an exceptionally good piece of head hunting because I was talked into taking a job that I would not otherwise have wanted.'

Like Dunne, Billingham believes that it is essential to maintain strong relationships with headhunters. 'I have always taken the approach of listening to what they have to say. Some people put the phone down on them, but I always take approaches and I also try to be helpful. If they ring and it's a not a job that I would want to do, I will always try and help them. It's good to have a reputation with head hunters as being someone who is worth contacting.'

While it is important to work with internal HR functions, recruitment consultants and headhunters to develop your career, you must always ensure that your career is taking the direction that you want it to take and not just the direction that *they* want it to take.

'Don't take a job that either head hunters or your internal HR try to push at you if it's not the right job for you,' says Scott Longhurst, group finance director of Anglian Water. 'Be disciplined in what you need as your next element of career experience in order to progress to the next level. If your organisation has a very big HR department, it can be a case of "we've got some vacancies and we need to fill them" – even if they have identified you as someone they want to develop.'

He continues: 'If the job you are offered is a diversion from what you feel in your heart is the right next role for you, be very cautious because your ambition, drive and mind-set are what will make you successful in the roles that you do. So don't do what you don't think is right for you.'

When you are weighing up whether to take a role or not, it is useful to keep your five-year plan in mind and assess whether that role will serve as a next step to helping you to achieve your ultimate goal. 'I think that's where head-hunters can be useful,' says Longhurst, 'because if you really want to make progress, staying within one organisation can sometimes be a mistake. People can become complacent about your career progression. On the other hand, getting a fresh perspective by moving to another business can be great for your career experience. If you do three years here and four years there early on in your career, you build up experience of different organisations, different cultures and different ways of working that can be hugely valuable for you when you take on a CFO role – particularly if that's in a multinational or a company with a particularly diverse workforce.'

Career hiccoughs

Almost all senior finance professionals will have had a career hiccough at some point – a job they shouldn't have taken, a project that didn't go as well as it should have done, or an employer that couldn't stay solvent. So a hiccough isn't something to get unnecessarily worried about – unless your own negligence caused the company's accounts to be restated, of course.

'If you joined a business and it went bankrupt, just front up to it,' says Mark Freebairn, partner and head of the financial management practice at executive search firm Odgers Berndtson. 'Everyone makes a mistake. Just don't make another one because then people start questioning your judgement. But if you did something that meant your integrity was questioned, that could be fundamentally damaging from a career perspective or it could be manageable, but it really depends on what the hiccough was and what the outcome was.'

Probably the most common career hiccough is moving to a new job and finding that it wasn't the role that you expected it to be, with the result that you really don't like the job and, possibly, the company. 'In that situation, if you truly believe you need to be in a different job, then leave,' advises Freebairn. 'There's absolutely no value in you wasting your time doing a job you're getting nothing out of and hating it rather than spending that time in a job you should be in.'

Young agrees that if you find yourself in this situation, it may be best to make a swift exit. 'If the cultural fit isn't right, you're not comfortable with it and you're not going to thrive in that environment, how are you going to be proactive?' she queries. 'If you are unhappy, how are you going to be curious about the business and able to offer insight? In that instance you're better off making a quick move – as long as it isn't another quick move in a long line of job hops. If you can explain the reasons behind the move, it shouldn't go against you.'

Nevertheless, both Freebairn and Young advise investigating first whether it is possible for the company to remedy the situation for you before you walk away. 'Give them a chance because if it can be fixed, it will be far better for your CV in the long term,' says Young. 'But if you can't fix it, you can walk away knowing you tried and that you can take that positive effort of doing so into your next interview.'

Dunne believes that good planning can help to keep career hiccoughs to a minimum because planning paves the way for moving onto the right job at the right time. 'Planning doesn't mean knowing what is going to happen, but preparing for opportunities that arise,' he says. 'If you're not clear on what your career agenda is, you may not be clear on when is the right time to move on. On one occasion I knew that I had been sufficiently long in a particular position so I made it clear to my then employer that I needed to move on inside the organisation or move out. But I did it in a constructive way that gave my organisation some notice and some space to think about whether or not they really did want to keep me and, if they did, how soon they would be able to do something for me.'

Again, this is why relationships matter enormously in career management. If you have previously invested in a relationship with your line manager or HR lead, and previously expressed what your career ambitions are, by the time you feel it's right to move on, you should be able to approach them about possible opportunities because you have laid the groundwork for a better conversation.

It is also key to avoid making assumptions, says Dunne. 'A lot of finance people presume that they will stay in their current role until they are promoted to the next level up. So they have a narrow base of expertise and their only option for promotion is landing their boss's job as opposed to getting a broad base of knowledge and experience that creates opportunities for them to be promoted into a wider range of roles. Too many finance people start narrow and assume that the only career direction they can take is securing their boss's job. I have been promoted to my boss's job on a number of occasions, but they haven't been the only opportunities that I have had.'

When your company goes under ...

Ian Kenyon, now CFO of Cancer Research UK, was headhunted for the group finance director role at struggling music retailer HMV in 2012. He was attracted to the role by the strength of the company's board – he had previously worked with the board chair – and the fact that the business was a well-known brand on the UK high street. Unfortunately, however, the business entered into administration just months after his arrival. 'I knew it was in trouble,' he recalls. 'But I think everyone thought that it was in a slightly better position than it actually was. I joined with a new CEO and we thought that we would have a couple of years to save it. Actually we just had five months.'

Looking back, and with the benefit of hindsight, Kenyon wonders if he could have done more due diligence, but says: 'I'm not certain I could have dug anything more out. What changed was that the banks, which for many years had supported the business, altered their views on our prospects because they were cleaning up their balance sheets. That's probably what pushed us into administration. But what I would say is that HMV is still here and there aren't many retailers that went into and came out of administration around that time. I still maintain it's a good business that has a great supplier base. It just had too much debt.'

Kenyon is clear that his brief spell at HMV did not have a negative impact on his CV, although he frequently has to field the question of why he decided to join the business in the first place. He learned a lot from the experience, however, including the importance of having a Plan B. 'For me, one of the key things a CFO needs to do is to make certain that there's a Plan B,' he says. 'You cannot just assume that Plan A will always work. So at HMV we were working hard to make certain that Plan A came off. Plan A didn't involve administration, but when we did go into administration, we were ready for that. Also, if I learned anything at HMV it is that the writing was probably on the wall for quite a long time beforehand. So you really do need to have a long-term vision and think through what the different scenarios might be. Finally, I learned about galvanising a team. Many of my team were working flat out through the weekend before we went into administration, trying to save the company. But they did it because they loved the organisation and they respected management.'

Passed over for promotion

One of the biggest crisis points in any finance professional's career is when he or she gets passed over for that big promotion – the one to partner or finance director, the one he or she felt certain had his or her name on it. Missing out on that promotion can be a really bitter blow, but if it happens to you, you can take comfort from the fact that you're not alone. Far from it, in fact.

'It happens all the time,' says Young. 'And if it happens to you, you need to ask yourself the question of why you're not making partner or finance director. What do you think they wanted in the finance director or partner that you didn't have? You have to get the mirror out, look at yourself and be really honest. Wherever possible, ask for detailed feedback from your employer, too.'

She advises undertaking a skills gap analysis to find out which skills you lack and then coming up with a development plan to address any skills gaps. She also suggests approaching the partner or finance director who was appointed and asking him or her for constructive feedback on what you can do to improve your chances of gaining that crucial promotion in the future.

This is a conversation that the partner or finance director should be willing to have, she says, because 'a brilliant leader needs to learn how to have those conversations with someone who is working for them and know when to set them free when the right external job comes up'. She adds: 'Good people work for good people, and when they are developed and set free at the right time, those good people can also come back. Developing them shows strong leadership.'

What Young doesn't necessarily advise is making an immediate decision to leave your organization on the grounds that you've lost out on the promotion. 'Every individual circumstance is different on that,' she says. 'Looking externally doesn't mean you have to go, although it could be the right decision if you think there is a better opportunity elsewhere. But if you've got a skills gap, you should try to fill it where you are – even if it's over a period of six months. That way you will have established the tool kit that you will need when you decide that you are ready to go for a partner or finance director position elsewhere.' She also warns that people who have missed out on being made partner can't expect to transfer directly into industry because 'it's not that easy'.

Campbell points out that, within practice, individuals are invited to join the partnership – they don't formally apply to become a partner. As a result, losing out on an anticipated partnership has a 'different flavour' to it from being rejected for an internal job in favour of someone else, she says. Nevertheless, it's still essential to undertake some in-depth personal analysis.

'If you're getting the message that partnership may not be for you, you need to probe why that is and what it is that someone is seeing in you or not seeing in you that is giving them that view,' she says. 'Then you need to test that more broadly to see if it's a shared view among others in the partnership. If it is, you need to find out what you need to change in terms of broadening your experience. So that might be taking on a secondment or working with new clients. Very often there is something you can do. I have seen senior managers who were passed over for partner once but were later promoted because they got good mentoring and support and access to new opportunities, which gave them a fresh perspective.'

Sometimes a firm will recognize that someone has the right skills and talent to be a partner, but that he or she needs to be exposed to different experiences, Campbell believes. 'Having said that, I think it is important to be able to tell someone honestly that partnership is not going to happen if we do know for sure. Then they can make a choice about what to do next.'

From Big Four partner to Fortune 500 CFO

Jack McGinnis is proof of the fact that you can transition to a career in industry from practice at any level – provided you have transferable skills.

He began his career at EY in the United States, where he worked in audit, mostly for financial services clients. He made partner in his mid-30s, after his relationship skills singled him out early in his career as someone who had great future potential. 'After about five or six years in public accounting, I started working for the clients of one of the managing partners in the office who served financial services businesses. He took me aside and said: "My clients called me to tell me what a great job you were doing on the account. They really like working with you."'

McGinnis says he was 'floored' by the managing partner's feedback. 'I couldn't believe it. Then he went on to say: "Hey, I'll tell you something. There are a lot of people around here who are accounting experts. We need those people because we're an accounting firm, but people who can make a connection with clients and are really good at client service are the people who are definitely partner potential. My advice to you is to keep doing what you're doing because you've got what it takes."'

Although McGinnis hadn't necessarily been focused on making partner at that point, getting this feedback from the managing partner had a tremendous impact on his career plan. 'At that point, being partner became a very strong goal of mine,' he says.

Once he had made partner, McGinnis had no particular plans to leave EY as he was happy at the firm. But in 2006, he took a call from a headhunter that was to set his career on a new course. The headhunter was looking for an audit partner with a strong technical background and experience in financial services to fill the senior role of controller with banking group HSBC in North America. At first, McGinnis said he wasn't interested but the headhunter persisted, so he agreed to meet with HSBC and was impressed by the bank's management team. He ended up taking the controller job; then four years later he was promoted to CFO for HSBC Bank in the United States. A couple of years after that, he was promoted again, to CFO for HSBC North America.

'I loved working for EY and never thought I would leave,' says McGinnis. 'But when you are pursued for an outstanding opportunity, it forces you to focus on the future and the pros and cons of the current path compared with other paths.

'When HSBC approached me, I was a fairly young partner and the public accounting industry was undergoing some dramatic changes in the post-Enron world. Sarbanes-Oxley legislation redefined what type of services the auditor could perform for its clients and there was a significant increase in the compliance aspects of an audit, which was the less enjoyable part of the job.

'The other consideration was that Securities and Exchange Commission audit rules required partner rotation after a number of years (typically five to seven). As I had small children, I was beginning to worry that I would need to move them several more times. But HSBC offered me a fantastic opportunity to settle back in my hometown of Chicago and raise our family. The irony is that HSBC moved its North American headquarters to New York a few years later and we moved when I was promoted to the US bank CFO role.'

Swapping practice for industry at this point in his career was not a huge shock to McGinnis. Very little surprised him about holding a senior financial role in the banking industry. 'This was largely due to the fact that during my 17 years at EY, I worked extremely closely with my clients and their teams and experienced first-hand many of the challenges they were facing,' he says. 'The areas of biggest learning early on were investor relations and certain aspects of interacting with regulators. Auditors do not spend much time with investors of clients and you really see the business through a different lens when you put yourself in the shoes of a large institutional investor.'

McGinnis was HSBC's chief accounting officer in North America when the global financial crisis struck in 2008. So he soon found himself in the thick of the action. 'As a result of the financial crisis, significant pressure was put upon the bank regulators and the boards of the banks,' he says. 'And finance management was central in terms of communicating clear information about operational results, the state of the balance sheet and capital adequacy. This was a very challenging time for management teams. There was pressure on the auditors as well, but the banks' management teams were on the front line during the crisis.'

After eight years at HSBC, McGinnis was approached by Morgan Stanley for the position of global controller. He decided to make the move. 'I loved working at HSBC but I wanted to advance beyond a regional CFO role,' he says. 'Realistically that would require a move from the US and that was not a good fit for our family. The Morgan Stanley global controller role allowed me an opportunity to join a US-headquartered firm where further advancement would not involve an international move.'

Then in 2016, McGinnis got his biggest break to date. He was appointed global CFO of Fortune 500 recruitment company ManpowerGroup, heading a worldwide finance function of around 1,000 people. He made the move out of financial services because it presented him with an opportunity to become a global CFO immediately, and after spending ten years in banking, he was ready for a change. 'There are very talented people in the banking industry and I miss working with many of them, but the banking regulatory compliance aspects of the industry are extremely time-intensive and I was interested in spending more time on business-related activities,' he explains.

Being the CFO of a Fortune 500 company is inevitably a pressurized job, but McGinnis believes that his background in public accounting helped to prepare him for his high-powered role. 'First and foremost I have an obligation to our shareholders, the board and the management team to report the financial results in a fair and accurate way,' he says. 'Public accounting prepares you well for this part of the job because you understand the extreme importance of public reporting accuracy. The CFO must have the confidence and trust of the board and the senior management team and they must be objective when analysing business performance and strategy.'

Looking back on his career, McGinnis is happy with the way it has turned out and about his decision to move into industry – although he will always have fond memories of life in practice. 'Public accounting is very special,' he says. 'What I mean by that is the people are fantastic and the partners are a great support for one another. If you have an issue with a client, you walk down a hall and you walk into another partner's office. Then you talk through the issue.'

'When you move into industry, you have great teams, but it is a little different. It's not like the partnership structure where there are groups of people who are all the same position, whether that's manager, senior manager or partner. There are very clear groups of where people are in their career. Move into industry and it's not quite like that. Also, in industry, you work with the same team constantly unlike public accounting where the team rotates to a large degree.' Being prepared for these differences is half the battle in adjusting to life in industry after working in practice, McGinnis believes.

Fortunately, however, moving into industry doesn't need to spell the end of association with the large professional services firms. 'The good news is you can work with the public accounting firms when you're with a large company,' McGinnis says. 'So you can still maintain very good relationships with the partners and staff on the engagement. There tends to be a very strong, mutual relationship on both sides.'

Networking and public speaking

If you want to make it to a senior position within finance, you need to be well networked. Don't worry though – networking doesn't have to be as scary as many people perceive it to be.

While there are many 'official' networking groups in existence, networking goes way beyond turning up at events where you know no one and hoping that you will find someone friendly to talk to as you help yourself to canapés and glasses of sparkling wine from silver trays.

At its most basic level, networking might simply involve having lunch with someone in another department or a contact from a previous employer. Or it might mean sending a message of congratulations via email or social media to a client or supplier who has just taken a new job. It might just be a matter of returning a call from a recruitment consultant or a headhunter, or agreeing to meet him or her for a coffee. Don't forget about friends and family either – people like the idea of doing business with people they know and trust – so make sure you talk to as many people as possible at your uncle's summer BBQ.

Ian Kenyon has made a point of maintaining a large and active network throughout his career. He has kept in particularly close contact with people that he worked with previously. 'Those relationships are incredibly valuable to you,' he says. 'And maintaining them doesn't take a huge amount of time out of your diary. They also provide you with the opportunity to learn from other people.'

'It is important that you network and that people know about you,' says David Tilston, former CFO of Innovia Group. 'Besides furthering your career, it increases the number of people you can ring and ask questions of. For example, if you've never done a bond issue before, you might want to call someone who has done a bond issue previously and ask questions like: What are the issues that caught you out?'

He adds that finance professionals need to devote time to networking throughout the course of their career – it isn't something they should only engage in when they are actively job hunting. 'It's important to evolve the network of people who know you and think well of you over time,' he says. 'As you carry on being recruited, you need to have a decent track record behind you and one that can be checked out and substantiated. The more people who say good things about you, the more likely you are to be seen as someone who is worth recruiting.

'Also, your network can essentially be a support network. So if something difficult is going on in your organisation, you may find it difficult to ask people within the organisation tricky questions. So to have some knowledgeable peers that you can have a confidential chat with can be helpful.'

You will find a host of good advice on networking on the internet if you search for it, but ultimately networking is really about putting basic communication skills into practice. If you are meeting someone new for the first time at an event, make sure you smile at him or her, listen, ask questions, respond to his or her answers, and be positive and open-minded. Don't make a beeline for the most senior figure in the room and stick resolutely by his or her side for the duration of the event; it won't make you popular with either the senior figure or anyone else who might be watching you and has the potential to influence your career. Ultimately, you never quite know who in life might send interesting opportunities your way, which is why you need to be respectful to everyone you meet.

LinkedIn can be another good way to network with your peers in other organizations and industries. Among the most popular LinkedIn groups for finance professionals are the Chief Financial Officer (CFO) Network, Accounting and Finance Professionals (AAFP) and Super CFO.

Networking is one way to raise your profile. Other ways include getting involved with your professional body, speaking at conferences, engaging in industry debates – with regulators, for example – and writing articles for trade magazines. If you are to speak at conferences, you will obviously need to hone your public speaking skills – something that will stand you in good stead given your other responsibilities if you hold a senior role in finance.

'You don't need to be a brilliant public speaker, but you've got to be an OK one,' says Tilston. 'If you're a listed company finance director, you're going to be doing results presentations to investors and analysts at least twice a year. So the communication aspect becomes more important. As you move up organisations and increase in seniority, your role will shift from doing (sitting at your desk and knocking out the numbers, followed by analysis) to communicating externally. This means you have to be comfortable putting your point across and dealing with people who disagree with your interpretation of what's going on in the market.'

Chapter end

What are the key takeaways from this chapter?

- Regardless of whether or not you have an accountancy qualification, the first ten years of your career are important, so you need to get as broad a base of experience as you can.
- If you want to move into industry from practice, you don't need to go as soon as you qualify, but it can be a good idea to move before you reach five years post-qualification.
- Always return the calls that you get from recruitment consultants and headhunters. Even if you don't want to change jobs now, having a good relationship with them will help you in the future.
- Don't stay in a job that you dislike – everyone has a career hiccough.
- Network constantly during the course of your career – good relationships lead to good opportunities.

Chapter 4

Being the business partner

The secret to my success
'I think the most pertinent attributes for me are drive and determination. It's striving to be the best, but it's also striving for the company you work for to be the best that it can be. It's both the personal drive and the drive for the organisation – and the team that you work with.'

Julie Brown, CFO, Smith & Nephew

The secret to my success
'I'm good at selecting a great team and I am able to show humility.'

Ian Kenyon, CFO, Cancer Research UK

These days, the word 'finance' is becoming increasingly synonymous with the phrase 'business partner' – at least in the English-speaking world. So within Anglo-Saxon companies, it is common for the CFO to have a seat on the board and to be involved in setting the corporate agenda and making big business decisions. In continental Europe, on the other hand, finance tends to be seen as more of a control function that has less involvement in the commercial operations of the company.

Nevertheless, there can obviously be exceptions within this broad categorization. There are examples of finance professionals who have decision-support roles in a cultural environment where finance is primarily seen as a control function. Also, there are examples of finance professionals who primarily have a control role in a cultural environment where finance tends to have more of a decision-support role. For example, regulators in the United Kingdom and the United States are making heavy demands of CFOs who work in financial services, which is increasing the amount of time they spend on compliance work – time that they could have otherwise spent on strategy or meeting with investors.

So, for those CFOs and finance functions where business partnering is seen as part of the job, what does being a business partner mean? Research by UK recruiter Robert Half in 2016[1] found that many CEOs and boards already expect the CFO to act as a strategic adviser who helps to grow the organization while also serving as 'the steward of the bottom line'.

'For me, being a business partner is about being able to identify emerging issues very early,' says Scott Longhurst, group finance director of Anglian Water. 'It's about really knowing your business, being able to identify what the key issues and key value drivers are and being able to scan the horizon for possible threats or opportunities. And it's being able to articulate that in a compelling story for the CEO and the board.'

'The best finance people really do understand the business,' observes Jack McGinnis, CFO of ManpowerGroup. 'They understand the financials, how the business makes its money and what the challenges are. The finance professionals that can balance those aspects with their day-to-day activities do really, really well.'

Expectations of CFOs as business partners are high now, and they are only going to increase further over the coming years. This is because CFOs will need to fulfil their obligations in an era of rapid technological change as automation and corporate digitization transform the finance function. There will be demand for greater operational efficiency in areas such as transactional processing and technical reporting, meaning finance professionals can focus their efforts on financial analysis and strategic planning instead of carrying out routine tasks. The result will be an exciting opportunity for strong, commercially minded finance functions to influence the direction that their organizations take in a competitive and rapidly changing world.

Relationships with other departments

It may seem obvious that to act as a business partner, the finance function needs to build relationships with the other key functions in the business, ranging from HR, procurement and operations through to sales and marketing. It is worth reiterating this point, however, since it is not unknown for the finance function to be jokingly dubbed the 'sales prevention department' in some organizations.

Significantly, there are a host of complications associated with doing business today – from the risks of political upheaval and cyberattack through to stringent regulations and the reputational risk associated with working with certain customers and suppliers. For this reason, the finance function needs to be well integrated with other functions in the organization so that it can access and interpret the data that they generate and turn this data into useful insight that will benefit the organization as a whole.

So budding CFOs will need to build strong and effective relationships with peers across other functions in their businesses. They will need to work with sales and marketing to understand how business targets are going to be reached and which customers present a significant financial risk as well as to ensure that meaningful cash flow forecasts are produced. Connecting with sales is particularly important since sales functions have a tendency to be over-optimistic about the revenues that they will generate. This can cause problems for the finance function, which has responsibility for ensuring that the business can meet its financial commitments over the weeks, months and years ahead. No CFO wants to be in the situation where an organization suffers a liquidity crisis because he or she has taken predictions from the sales department at face value.

The budding CFO will also need to work with procurement to ensure that costs are being managed effectively and that suppliers are offering attractive terms. He or she needs to work with operations to ensure that the organization's product or service is being produced in a cost-effective manner and customer satisfaction scores are high. And he or she needs to work with HR to understand the human capital of the business – for example, is the business structured in the optimum way? Is there a need for training to improve productivity? How many redundancies may need to be made in light of an upcoming acquisition or forecast downturn in the economy?

Communication is what underpins all relationships – both within the business world and outside it. Finance professionals who want to build strong relationships with people in other functions need to make an effort to get to know them, talk to them regularly and share information that will help them to understand the implications of their forecasts and activities. By sitting down with their colleagues, they can help them to understand how they are contributing to the organization's success – or lack of it. It is only when all functions have a shared understanding as to where the business is at, that steps can be taken to improve performance.

Another consideration is that if the relationship between finance and other functions is to really work well, that relationship needs to work well at several levels within the organization. It can't just be the CFO and the head of procurement who talk regularly to each other, for example. The relationship also needs to work at levels below head of department. And if that relationship isn't working, the two heads of department should communicate the importance of it to their teams to ensure that the flow of information and the support that exists is at the level that the organization needs to succeed.

'Building relationships between various functions is absolutely critical,' says David Tilston, former CFO of Innovia Group. 'It puts you in a position where you can try to make sure that there is some consistency of understanding of financial performance and operational performance across the different divisions.

'You can think of the finance function as the scorekeeper, but part of the scorekeeping function is going out and explaining the scores to the different departments and flagging up how the scores can be improved to the benefit of all.'

Working with the CEO

The relationship between the CEO and the CFO is one of the most important and powerful relationships in any organization. The CEO is the person with the vision, the person who sets the strategy for where the organization will be heading and, crucially, they also set the tone at the top – for good or for bad.

But CEOs cannot operate as an island. The decisions they take can have far-reaching consequences, so they need to be able to base their decision-making on reliable – and, often confidential – information, particularly information regarding the financial performance of the company and the risks that it faces. Since the CFO has access to most of the critical information that the CEO needs, this makes him or her the CEO's natural business partner.

'A CFO's relationship with the CEO is crucial,' says Longhurst. 'The CFO has got to have respect for the CEO and the CEO has got to have respect for their CFO. They have got to be able to trust each other and they've got to make sure they're both on board with the strategic direction of the business.'

While analysts, investors, the media and the board will judge a CEO by a range of criteria, the financial performance of the company will normally be the single most important criterion on which formal and informal assessments of the CEO will be based. So CEOs will be expected to deliver on a range of financial targets that include revenue, profit, cost per sale, free cash flow and earnings per share. They may be tasked with following an M&A or a divestment strategy. And their mandate may include turning around a function, a division or – as is often the case – an entire company.

If CEOs are under pressure to deliver, what do they themselves want from their CFO? Usually, they will want their CFO to act as a 'critical friend'. Let's start with the 'friend' part first. For a CEO and a CFO to be 'friends' with each other, they need to have a strong relationship and personalities that fit. When a CEO and a CFO do not get on, the relationship cannot work and the best thing that a CFO can do in this situation is to get out of it as quickly as possible while keeping his or her professional dignity and reputation intact. Otherwise, the CFO could end up having to make an exit at a time and in a way that is not of his or her choosing. There is a caveat, though, and that is the nature of the CEO's own situation in the company. If that is looking perilous – turnover of CEOs tends to be high – then it might be worth the CFO sitting tight in the hope that the situation improves with a change of leadership at the top. Alternatively, the CFO may even have an opportunity to bid for the CEO job.

But assuming that the CEO and the CFO do fundamentally get along, the CFO needs to build a strong relationship with the former. This will involve the CFO taking the time to understand the CEO's vision for the organization and approach to leadership as well as getting to know him or her on a personal level – perhaps by having lunch together or by asking about his or her family, interests and hobbies. The CEO's job can be incredibly lonely, so CEOs will usually appreciate having a senior colleague to confide in. It goes without saying that what the CEO tells the CFO can go no further; the discretion of a CFO must be paramount.

Once the respect and trust of the CEO has been gained, CFOs need to make it clear that they are available to act as a 'sounding board'. The CEO and the CFO can have a dialogue and bounce ideas around with each other in a safe environment. This can be particularly valuable if sensitive decisions need to be made – for example, decisions around large restructuring or redundancy programmes. In this context, the CFO should also be able to influence the CEO – by using financial analysis if necessary – to weigh up different scenarios and consider different courses of action.

The old adage 'two heads are better than one' comes into play here since brainstorming with the CFO will often enable the CEO to come up with a strategy that is more suitable for the business than the one he or she originally had in mind. 'By discussing an issue together, the CEO-CFO team will often come up with a solution that is better than either of them could have come up with individually,' says Tilston. 'Being flexible enough to kick things around and work well with a CEO is part and parcel of being a successful business partner.'

Working with entrepreneurs

Entrepreneurial leaders tend to be very different leaders from CEOs who came up the corporate route. For a start, it's likely that they will have founded the business and that they continue to own a significant share of it – possibly the majority – along with family members as well as 'outside' investors. Since they have overseen the growth of the organization from a tiny start-up right through to a significant enterprise, they will almost certainly have a great passion for what they do and clear ideas about what they want. They are probably also used to getting their own way – most of the time.

While they will be strong-minded, and this can make them challenging to work for, most successful entrepreneurs appreciate that they need to surround themselves with trusted advisers – and that they should heed those advisers' advice – if they want their businesses to succeed. So a good entrepreneurial leader will not necessarily be any more difficult to work with than a good corporate CEO – and, in some respects, the opportunities that come with working for an entrepreneur may be greater because the business is fast-growing and dynamic, and – if it is not a listed company – it can focus more on the long term because it is not under pressure to deliver short-term results to shareholders.

Entrepreneurs tend to be 'big picture' visionaries, however, rather than the analytical, detail-oriented individuals that a lot of finance people are, which can make life interesting for their CFOs.

'The challenge for entrepreneurs is that usually we are very good at certain things and detail is rarely one of those things,' says Brad Sugars, the founder of business coaching franchise ActionCOACH. 'So we, as entrepreneurs, have to understand that the people on our team are there to do a job. If we wanted to do it, we'd do it. But most entrepreneurs don't want to do the detailed stuff.'

Having said that, Sugars is quite clear that 'you don't let accountants and lawyers run the company, you let them give you advice'. But while he wants his CFO to give him the best advice possible to make an entrepreneurial decision, he doesn't necessarily take that advice because – in his view – it might not be the course of action that is preferable for the company at that time. Sugars takes financial matters into account during his decision-making but he also factors in marketing, sales and any other considerations that may be relevant to business performance.

The impulsiveness and unpredictability of entrepreneurs can make them frustrating bosses for CFOs, which is why any finance professional who chooses to work with an entrepreneur needs to accept that his or her professional life will probably be much more eventful than if he or she took a job with a large corporate. 'We are far more risky than a finance person would usually want us to be,' Sugars acknowledges. 'Finance people would like us to have 12 months' worth of costs sitting in cash in the bank and sometimes we want to go out and buy another business.'

Ian Kenyon worked as group finance director of carpet retailer Carpetright earlier in his career. Founded in 1988 by Phil Harris – now Lord Harris of Peckham – it currently has 460 stores across the UK with additional stores in Belgium, Holland and the Republic of Ireland. Although the business was listed on the London Stock Exchange in 1993, its identity was very much shaped by the personality of its cash flow-focused entrepreneurial founder, who served as chief executive for twenty-four years until 2012. 'Lord Harris knew the numbers inside out, back to front,' says Kenyon. 'He had this innate ability to know how much the rent was at every shop.'

If influencing skills matter for a CFO who reports to the CEO of a public company, they matter even more when the CEO is a strong entrepreneurial leader. Knowing when to pick your battles is particularly important when you are dealing with an entrepreneur, so you will want to save your energy for a topic that you feel passionate about. 'I never disagreed with Phil in public,' notes Kenyon, 'but I may have put forward an alternative view in private.' While he was at Carpetright, Kenyon also learned the importance of being able to work with the non-executive directors on the board to support and influence the CEO.

Echoing Sugars' point, Kenyon says that CFOs who work with entrepreneurs should remember that the entrepreneurs hired them for their financial acumen and will therefore want them to manage the organization's finances. Nevertheless, the CFOs will need to invest some time in building up the entrepreneur's confidence in them before they will be trusted as strategic partners. No entrepreneur is going to risk allowing someone he or she has just hired to destroy a lifetime of achievement overnight. 'It's very important that you establish your credibility before you start trying to make any changes,' Kenyon observes.

Working with private equity firms

Many finance professionals carve out very successful careers working for businesses that are owned by private equity firms. It is important to note, however, that the culture of a private equity-owned organization tends to be very different from that of a publicly listed company, in the sense that the investors take a much more active interest in the running of the business than the shareholders in a listed company.

The business model of private equity firms is based on their pooling capital from institutional investors and high-net-worth individuals so that they can invest majority stakes in underperforming companies with a view to turning them round to achieve high growth. Ultimately, their aim is to make a profit on the business after a few years by selling out when the business is in a better shape than when they bought it, either by listing the business on the stock market or by selling it to another buyer. So during their period of ownership, they work with the business's management team to set strategic direction and drive operational improvements.

Since private equity firms want to make a good rate of return on their investment, they are usually very well versed in the language of finance. They also demand a high level of visibility into financial matters, particularly the cash position of the business– so they set great store by regular cash flow forecasts, for example – and they are interested in how different scenarios will impact on business performance. As a result, private equity firms often see the CFO as the first point of contact if they have a concern about a business matter.

'A good CFO in a private equity environment speaks the language of the shareholders, who will be very financially biased, but they will also be able to translate what the management team is saying into a language that the private equity firms understand,' explains Longhurst. His business, Anglian Water Services, was a publicly listed company before it was bought by a group of private equity investors in 2006.

'Also, you need to be on top of your numbers in board meetings and you've got to understand the business,' he continues. 'The private equity firms have analysts who will have pored over the reports. So they will ask far more in-depth questions than you would get from directors on the board of a publicly listed company.'

In addition to the private equity investors, Anglian's board includes independent non-executive directors who look closely at the operational dynamics of the business and matters such as health and safety. So the role of the CFO in this context is to ensure that the interests and concerns of all the directors are covered off and that the private equity investors on the board are aware of their legal responsibilities as the owners of a regulated utility company.

Working with clients

Like their peers who work in the finance functions of companies and not-for-profit organizations, accountants who work in practice also like to describe themselves as business partners. In fact, the moniker is a perfectly reasonable term to use since the big professional services firms (besides many smaller ones) work closely with their clients on a whole variety of issues that range from how much tax they should pay through to how they can protect their IT systems from cyberattacks. As a result, their professional staff spend a large amount of time working on client sites and may even feel that they know their client organizations better than they know their own.

Since professional services is a client-facing environment and professional services firms need to keep winning work so that they can stay in business and grow, the ability to work in partnership with clients is a critical skill for accountants who work in practice. In their early days, trainee auditors need to be able to build relationships with the clients that they work with so that they can get the information and the knowledge they need to do their jobs more effectively. As they rise through their organizations, they will be increasingly expected to contribute to the process of winning additional work from both existing and new clients.

To do this, they need to be able to demonstrate that they have a sound understanding of the nature of the client organizations that they are working with - the opportunities and challenges that they face and any political or regulatory complexities that may be involved. Hence senior leaders in practice often prefer to describe their approach to new business as 'building relationships' rather than using the straightforward - and less glamorous-sounding - term 'selling'.

'I understand that one of my responsibilities as a partner is to grow our business and that's paramount', says Rachel Campbell, global head of people, performance and culture at KPMG International. 'But I don't think of my role as being one of a saleswoman *per se*. I think my role is to build deep, meaningful relationships with clients, which enables me to really get to the root of what's going on their mind. Again, it's lots of questions, lots of exploration. You never feel like you're walking in with a product, but rather you're working with a client to help them solve challenges and issues that they have.

'The route to being a successful partner is relationship-driven. That said, you can have great relationships over a cup of tea but never build the relationship up beyond that. It's about having the confidence to help your client. That's less about selling skills and it's more about having a good understanding of business and business issues as well as a good understanding of what expertise your firm can bring to bear. I have real confidence because I know my organisation and I know the skills and capabilities that my fellow partners have.

'It's not about selling, it's about helping people buy. It's about building a relationship where they want to seek you out and where they turn with the next challenge and the next problem. It's a much more relationship-driven activity.'

Working in not-for-profit

Even if you work for an organization that isn't technically a business – that is, it doesn't make profits – you should still be a business partner. CFOs who work for a not-for-profit or governmental organization may not need to worry about earnings before interest, taxes, depreciation and amortization (EBITDA), but they still have a responsibility to ensure that funds – which may come via taxpayers or supporters or both – are spent effectively so that the maximum amount of money is spent on the cause itself and not on administrative arrangements.

They may also need to be involved in cost-cutting, redundancy and restructuring programmes as well as in securing additional funding for the organization from external sources. And while there may be a board of trustees, rather than a board of directors, to consider, a CFO still needs to understand how to advise and influence them so that the best investment decisions are made. The hours aren't necessarily much shorter than those worked by CFOs in the corporate sector either. 'You still end up working at the weekend,' says Kenyon. 'You still end up doing the normal late night every so often.'

Perhaps the main difference is that CFOs in the not-for-profit sector work towards very different 'business' goals than their peers in the private sector. Instead of trying to help the business to generate more revenue by selling more shampoo to emerging markets or to double profits through investment in the development of a market-leading fintech platform, they are more likely to be helping to find the money for a major new research programme, ensuring that buses run to schedule or reducing the number of children who die from malaria in sub-Saharan Africa. Often they find that they are working to far longer time frames than CFOs in corporates – results are measured over multiples of years, if not decades, rather than 24-month periods.

'Research is not something that can be measured over the short term,' explains Ian Kenyon, CFO of Cancer Research UK, the UK's largest fundraising charity, which raises over £600 million a year. 'Some of the research work we fund may not demonstrate value for many, many years. So what we fund is important, but we don't get an immediate correlation to positive benefit.'

Reputation is also something that the CFOs of not-for-profit organizations need to consider. While reputation also matters greatly to corporates, it takes on another dimension in not-for-profit organizations, since stakeholders have extremely high moral expectations about where the organization's funding should come from and what it should do with the money that it gets.

'We don't sell a product,' says Kenyon. 'We sell a belief, we sell the vision that we will beat cancer at some stage. We are given money to spend on research. People trust us to spend that on the right research and they trust us to raise it in the right way. Also, our brand is a global research organisation. So we have to make certain that we root what we do in evidence. If we're going to have a position on tobacco, which we do have, is this position on tobacco rooted in evidence? We can demonstrate with objective evidence that tobacco has an impact on cancer.'

The parameters in which a not-for-profit CFO must operate can add an extra dimension to the job, Kenyon acknowledges. 'Sometimes it can make it harder to influence internally, particularly when you spend about £450 million a year on research, as we do. If we cut £1 million out of the cost base, it means that we can spend £451 million on research. That's not a great change in substantive terms. On the other hand, if you take out £1 million from your cost base in a corporate and it drives your profit up by 10 per cent, that's quite significant.

'The metric for me is how much we've got to spend on research. So, internally, we have to keep making certain that people are aware of efficiency ratios. This is so we can assure our supporters and others that we have the right ratio of expenditure on fundraising and administration compared to research.'

Ultimately, the challenges of having a senior finance role in the not-for-profit sector are just as significant as the challenges of having a senior role in the corporate sector. Finance professionals who see moving into the not-for-profit sector as part of their career plan won't necessarily find that the pace is slower or that the hours are fewer. The pay will normally be less, though, but the compensation will be that their new colleagues are extremely passionate about what they do.

'Cancer Research UK has an engagement score in the high 80s [out of 100],' says Kenyon. 'You don't usually get that in a corporate and that's because we have people who are so committed to the cause. So if you want to work for a not-for-profit organisation, I would say to look for a cause that you can commit yourself to. I'm fascinated by the whole cancer story and the cancer journey.'

A spell in a large charity or not-for-profit organization can also provide aspiring finance leaders with valuable skills and experience that they can take with them if they go on to roles in the commercial sector – such as influencing skills and experience of long-term planning. In the past, members of Kenyon's team have left to join UK retailer Marks & Spencer and pharmaceutical giant GlaxoSmithKline, both FTSE 100 constituents. Overall, working for Cancer Research UK is a 'fantastic job', says Kenyon. 'Yes, you compromise a little bit on the salary, but you have the opportunity to do something you love.'

Presenting to the board

Presenting to the board is a big part of a CFO's job, so it's an area that ambitious finance professionals should try to gain experience in as they progress in their career. As with most things in life, preparation is key to making a successful presentation to the board, as is taking some time to reflect on what your key message will be.

'The worst thing you could do at a board meeting is turn up with loads of paper, dump it on the table and say, "These are the results," but not give any insight or a commercial perspective,' explains Longhurst. 'You need to think about the journey that you're going to take the board on and make sure there aren't any surprises. You're absolutely lost if you go into a board meeting and tell them something that comes completely out of the blue.' If a CFO is presenting on a particularly complex issue, Longhurst's advice is to build up the picture over a series of board meetings rather than trying to cover the issue in one session.

Geraldine Matchett, CFO of Royal DSM, uses her presentations to the company's supervisory board to bring the company's figures to life. 'I'm translating the numbers into insights that enable the board to steer the company,' she says. 'It is about more than just trends and ratios. It is my responsibility to identify the few key messages that are the most relevant. Without the privilege of time spent within a company, it is very difficult for board members to capture a good picture of how the businesses are doing from reading the financials. My role is to help provide context, and it is highly appreciated.' Nevertheless, she adds: 'The shorter and clearer the presentation, the more thought and time it takes to prepare.'

Tilston believes that it is the role of the CFO to address important, but unpopular issues. 'You have to understand what topics are of interest to the board members and sometimes you will have to tell them about topics that may not be of interest to them, but that they need to know about, nevertheless. For example, a sales-driven CEO will want to know about sales figures, but he or she may also need to know that if the business grows too quickly, it could suffer a liquidity crisis that limits its ability to operate as a going concern.'

CFOs also need to manage the way in which their team members appear before the board. According to Tilston, good CFOs will prep their team before a board meeting. They may also make helpful pointers during the meeting itself. 'In the past, I have asked questions of the team who are presenting to get them to make the right points,' he says. 'Rather than me saying: "The answer is x because of a, b and c," I will say: "Have you given any consideration to a, b and c and what the implications might be?"'

When the CFOs are present at the board meeting, they can act as a safety net to prevent their team from tripping up in front of the board – something that could potentially be career-limiting for both the members of the finance team and their CFO. 'If your team gets into trouble and messes up in front of the board, it's fundamentally down to you,' says Tilston. 'It reflects badly on the CFO.'

He continues: 'Ask to see the presentation before the team goes into the board so that you know what they will say and you don't disagree with it. You don't want your subordinates coming out with something you fundamentally disagree with. Having to shoot them down in front of your board colleagues doesn't look good.'

Relationships with investors

The term 'investor relations' refers to the company's communication with its investors. It is essential that companies communicate well with their investors – whether those are equity shareholders, bondholders, private equity investors or institutional investors – if they want to gain cost-effective access to capital and, in the case of listed companies, to maintain and increase the value of their share price. In addition, the greater focus on corporate governance since the financial crisis and the rise of 'activist shareholders' who want to influence the behaviour of companies is also increasing the importance of investor relations.

Typically, the investor relations function reports to the CFO or to the company's PR or corporate communications department. It takes charge of written communications with investors in the form of briefings and the investor relations sections of company websites and annual reports. It is also involved in the organization of annual general meetings (also known as shareholder meetings), conference call updates and one-to-one briefings with investors.

As the financial figurehead of the company, the CFO is expected to play a pivotal role in investor relations. That is because investors will look to him or her to provide an accurate assessment of the company's financial performance and future prospects. Major institutional investors, in particular, want reassurance that they are deriving value from their significant investments in a company, so they will often expect to be able to speak to the CFO in person, and in private, if need be.

Relationships with investors are built on trust, Tilston says. 'Investors – as well as analysts and banks – want to be able to trust the management team.

They want to be able to rely on the information that the management team is giving them with regard to how the business is going to develop. So the CFO needs to be able to openly explain the key drivers of the business so that analysts can compile their own reasonable forecasts for the future.'

He adds: 'Sometimes, when they are confronted with a particularly ambitious, growth-focused CEO, investors draw comfort from the CFO. They expect the CFO to have sufficient influence with the CEO to keep his or her feet on the ground.'

From the CFOs' point of view, working with investors should be one of the most interesting and enjoyable parts of their job. 'I like doing investor relations and meeting with investors in the company and helping them to understand how the business makes the money that it does and how the business model works,' says Jack McGinnis, CFO of ManpowerGroup. 'I like being able to answer their questions about competitors and what we think are differentiators for our business. That's also very energising.' McGinnis also emphasizes the importance of communicating with investors. 'Transparency saves them valuable time in understanding the business,' he explains.

Investors are not just individuals and institutions that have a share of ownership in the company. They can also be debt investors that have lent the company money. So while private equity firms own Anglian Water Services, it also has debt investors that hold bonds in the company. As a result, CFO Scott Longhurst has to be proactive about managing relationships with those investors. 'A lot of very big companies hold our corporate bonds so it is crucial to manage those relationships effectively,' he says. 'You want to know all your big investors, whether they are bondholders or shareholders.'

The prospect of meeting with investors can be daunting for a newly promoted CFO, but Matchett says that preparation will help make it easier. 'The first time is undoubtedly the most difficult,' she explains. 'But it's always about good preparation – making sure that you've spent enough time identifying the few key messages and that you've done your homework on the tricky questions that are likely to be asked, so that you have a plan on how you deal with them.

'Some analysts and brokers can be helpful by sharing the questions they have been asked by investors so that you can prepare for the investor meetings. You can even have a dry run with one or two of them so that when you meet the investors you are not trying to formulate your thoughts on certain subjects for the first time. A good investor relations team is a good sparring partner too, although they are less able than analysts and brokers to put the answers in context of what other similar companies are saying.'

Relationships with the auditor, banks and credit rating agencies

Besides investors, the other external stakeholders that a CFO needs to have strong relationships with are the company's external audit firm, banks and credit rating agencies. All of these stakeholders have an impact on a company's ongoing financial viability and how it is perceived in the marketplace.

When it comes to learning how to handle these external stakeholders, Matchett advises sitting in as many meetings as possible with them when you're in a junior role within the company. 'Before you have to stand up and do it yourself, there's a lot of benefit to be gained from going along to meetings with other people and observing how they handle discussions,' she says.

Longhurst says that CFOs build strong relationships with external stake-holders by investing time in them. 'It is important to work well with your external audit partner and ensure that they can be pragmatic,' he says. 'Clearly your auditor has to be independent and objective, but you want an audit partner you can get on with. If, having tried to resolve the issue, you still don't get on with them, it may help to speak to the senior rela-tionship partner at whichever firm you use to see if there is another audit partner whom you can have the right chemistry with. You want someone who understands your business and whom you can work effectively with, albeit they are fully independent of the business.'

With banks, Longhurst says that it's a matter of being able to call on the right people when issues arise. 'We've got about four or five core banks and I will spend a fair amount of time working on those relationships. When I'm in London, I'll meet them with our treasurer, just to identify where they can help us and what their understanding is of the general business environment.'

Matchett says that managing relationships with rating agencies is quite similar to managing relationships with investors and shareholders. 'You may share more forward-looking information with them than you would share with investors, as they are bound to non-disclosure agreements,' she explains. 'In some circumstances it may be necessary to share budget indications, for example.'

Since companies typically go through the process of obtaining a credit rating when they want to raise debt, CFOs may first use a bank to advise them on how they should liaise with the credit rating agencies. The bank will be able to let the CFOs know what kinds of questions they should expect and help them to handle and follow up on the questions they receive. Then, as time moves on, it will be the job of the company's treasury team to become familiar with the different ratios that matter to the rating agencies and establish a regular dialogue with them to avoid any surprises, such as the company announcing an unexpected fall in profits or the agency suddenly downgrading the company's credit.

Media relations

Talking to the media is something many CFOs try to do as little as possible, but it is something that they need to do if they work for a listed company – when the annual results come out, if at no other time.

Matchett's recommendation for dealing with the media is to get training and coaching on how to talk to journalists, since the objectives of the media often differ significantly from those of financial analysts. For instance, she says that TV journalists are looking for statements and not explanations, so they appreciate responses that start with a conclusion or opinion. Only when they have time will they also seek to know the rationale. Training will help a CFO to understand the areas that journalists are likely to hone in on and the questions they may pose. It will also equip CFOs with useful sentences to help them avoid having to answer unwelcome questions. 'Handling the media is not something that can easily be done well without regular practice,' Matchett concludes.

'My own personal view is don't get involved in the media aspect unless you have to,' says Longhurst, 'because you can go off on a tangent very quickly. When I was in a publicly listed company, I got involved in the media when we were doing our interim and annual results. In that situation, you have to be very clear on your messaging around the results and what the implications of those results are.'

Managing cost-saving programmes

If you have ambitions to become a CFO, the chances are that you will end up overseeing at least one major cost-saving/restructuring programme during the course of your career – and possibly many of them. Restructuring programmes are a mixed blessing for finance leaders. On the one hand, they are a lot of work and they can result in a lot of negative feeling within the company if job losses are involved. On the other hand, they put finance right at the heart of the company and they are a great opportunity for a finance leader to demonstrate his or her credentials as a strategist and a change leader.

The reality is that, depending on how they go, restructuring programmes can make or break a finance leader's career. So how is it possible to increase the chances of a programme being considered a success?

'Invest in creating a clear plan from the beginning, recommends Smith & Nephew CFO Julie Brown, who has the experience of leading multibillion dollar cost-saving and restructuring programmes. 'Decide on the level of ambition you can reach for – reach high – and create a clear plan about the major source of the savings, the major sources of opportunity. Always go for the big processes, big opportunities and big enablers like systems. If you use the right levers, the cost savings will be delivered because you've changed the underlying process and the underlying capability of the organisation.

'My second piece of advice would be to set up a programme management office (PMO) that manages the programme and dissects it into deliverable chunks with timelines and goals and the amount of savings associated with each of those major milestones.

'Thirdly, appoint the right leaders for the work streams – people who are going to be capable of taking the organisation to the next level. Then use the PMO to track the progress and execution against the plan.

'Finally, communicate, communicate, communicate. Restructuring programmes leave people feeling very uncertain about their position in the organisation and very uncertain about their jobs. The only thing you can do is be completely honest with people, communicate what's happening, ensure you keep people involved and informed and go through the programme as quickly as you can so that you can execute on it and people have certainty as quickly as possible.'

Restructuring programmes can be a good opportunity to advance not only your own career but also the careers of the finance professionals within your team. Brown puts it this way: 'Somebody once said to me: "Never waste the opportunity of a good transformation to develop your talent." It is true that people develop huge amounts of skill and confidence in their own abilities by leading some of these programmes. At the end of it, they can turn round and say: "I saved a billion dollars or I saved 250 basis points on the margin." Being able to say that can make people's careers.'

The future of finance

According to EY's 2016 report, *The DNA of the CFO*, nearly half (47 per cent) of CFOs are concerned that their current finance function does not have the right mix of capabilities to meet the demands of their organization's future strategic priorities.

This is not surprising given the way finance is likely to change over the next decade or so. As more processes become automated and finance functions make greater use of robotic process automation and artificial intelligence to do tasks that were previously carried out by humans, there will be more pressure on CFOs and their teams to evolve their roles so that they become providers of valuable strategic input to their organizations. Accounts payable, travel and expenses and general ledger work are among the areas where robotic process automation is most likely to happen in the near term, according to Deloitte's 2015 report, *The Robots are Coming*.[2]

In the world of audit, workflow automation, data analytics and artificial intelligence will change how audits are done – for example, the 'sampling' technique will disappear as advances in technology enable the analysis of an entire set of accounting journals, not just samples of those journals. As a result, it will be possible to search for anomalies or odd patterns of transactions in vast swathes of data. Predictive technologies based on past data may be used to run 'what if' scenarios for the future and, thanks to ever faster computer systems, smarter software tools and blockchain, we will probably move to real-time audits where transactions are audited as they happen. Some of the big firms are also investigating how drones can be used to do the inventory checks that are a crucial part of an audit.[3]

Finance functions are already used to dealing with data, but over the coming years, they will have to get even more used to it. As organizations digitize more of what they do, they will generate increasingly large amounts of data – and they will need the finance function to help them analyse that data.

'The internet of things will be throwing off data from every object on our factory floor and every product we sell,' says Rohit Talwar, futurist and editor and co-author of *The Future of Business*.[4] 'We'll be drowning in data. So the ability to use that data and extract value from it for the organisation will be a key role for finance.'

Heightened focus on data could mean greater demand for forensic accountants, Talwar predicts. 'Today there's a risk that a lot of things could slip through the cracks because we don't audit every transaction,' he says. 'But if we're auditing and monitoring every transaction, suddenly all sorts of possibilities are created.'

Talwar produced the research report, *100 Drivers of Change for the Global Accountancy Profession*,[5] for accountancy bodies ACCA and IMA. The report identified intelligent systems and big data as being one of five key forces driving change in the accountancy profession, along with the pressure on the profession to improve its public image and provide a more transparent picture of a company's health and prospects; an increased regulatory burden; the continued globalization of accounting standards; and growing expectations that the CFO and accounting function should be more deeply involved with core aspects of value creation in the organization – from strategic decision-making to the design of new revenue models.

Going forward, Talwar believes that the finance function will need to become more 'user-friendly', more strategically aware and more collaborative than it is today. 'There's a low level of literacy around finance among many business managers,' he says. 'So there's a role there for finance professionals to explain to the business managers what the data means to them and how they should read the information on their financial reports and balance sheets. Finance professionals need to be able to say to their business: How can we help you to understand the numbers, use them to generate value and make smarter business decisions?'

He also believes that finance has a big role to play in terms of understanding the financial implications of the platforms and technologies of tomorrow and experimenting with new pricing models, new payment tools, new approaches to valuation and new methods of funding.

Training programmes for new accountants will change in light of the new responsibilities they will have, Talwar argues. 'There will always be a need to understand the technical skills of accounting. But more and more, I think those courses will need to address strategy, technology and doing business in a globalised economy. Finance could and should become much more of a forward-thinking, research-driven, strategic function than it is today.'

Chapter end

What are the key takeaways from this chapter?

- To be a business partner in industry, a finance professional must build relationships with the other key functions in the business, ranging from HR, procurement and operations through to sales and marketing.
- Finance professionals in practice act as business partners by helping to solve their clients' problems. So they need to be able to build up strong relationships with the clients they work with.
- Finance professionals who work in not-for-profit organizations usually work to longer time frames than their peers in corporates and their success is measured according to how much money the organization has to spend on its cause.
- It is crucial that CFOs build up a strong relationship with their company's investors. Working with investors is actually one of the most interesting aspects of the job.
- The finance professionals of the future will need to have strong analytical and strategic skills because their role will be more about evaluating data – and less about actually producing it.

Chapter 5

Leadership and management

The secret to my success

'I have drive and resilience and I want to be successful. I also have a fear of failure so I want to be on top of what I'm doing.'

Scott Longhurst, group finance director, Anglian Water

The secret to my success

'I am really fortunate that my wife and kids have never let me get carried away with my own self-importance. They called me the UFO as I was of no earthly use!'

Andrew Bonfield, group finance director, National Grid

CFOs in large companies or senior partners in professional services firms have a huge leadership and management job. They may directly and indirectly oversee the activities of hundreds, if not thousands, of people. As a result, they must be able to attract good people to work for them, lead and inspire those people, and manage them in a way that gets the best out of them. They need to be a coach, a mentor and a sponsor, and they need to see developing the next generation of finance talent as one of their most important responsibilities.

It is not just the management team and the board that will expect a CFO to be focused on developing the next generation. Investors are increasingly interested in the sustainability of business models, so they will also want to know how finance talent is managed. What, then, does it mean to be a good leader and manager in the context of the finance function?

'It depends on the size of the organisation, but in a medium-to-large business a good CFO focuses on leading, enabling and motivating their direct reports,' says Karen Young, director of Hays Senior Finance. 'They delegate to them and they have an open line of communication. They also have clear individual development plans with each of their direct reports.'

Where CFOs fall down in the leadership and management stakes is when they start interfering with the activities of the people who don't report to them directly but who report to line managers lower down the chain of command. Problems can also arise if they allow themselves to get too bogged down in the detail, Young believes. 'They are so busy trying to manage everyone that they don't get the chance to lead. Also, their leadership will be weakened if they tolerate bad behaviour and poor performance.'

The finance leaders who were interviewed for this book emphasized that they have built up strong teams to support them. To build these strong teams, they have hired and developed finance professionals with specialist expertise and they have actively sought out outstanding individuals who are far better at doing their jobs than the finance leader in question would ever be.

'You need a very disciplined hiring process,' says David Tilston, former CFO of Innovia Group. 'Motivating and retaining people is all about continuous development and improvement, and moving people into different roles to help them broaden their careers so that they see you are interested in them.'

He warns that it is a bad idea to find good people, place them in a role, then leave them there and forget about them. 'In my team I want to have motivated people who are developing and could go on to other roles, even if there is a risk of losing them,' he says. 'If they get poached, I would rather they went to the next company and we parted on good terms and they appreciated being helped along in their careers. But if they are motivated, being challenged and getting access to new opportunities internally, then hopefully you will hang on to them anyway.'

CFOs who want to be recognized as great managers and leaders must show that they have confidence in the abilities of their team and be willing to let them get on with the job at hand. 'I've got technical experts in financial reporting, tax and treasury,' says Scott Longhurst, group finance director of Anglian Water. 'I trust those people and I give them the autonomy to do what they need to do. Then I just dip in and out to keep on top of what's happening.

'I also think it's good to have a trouble shooter, someone who may have qualified within the past five years who works closely with me on ad hoc issues. It makes my job easier and they get a huge amount out of it. But you have to move them on every two or three years because they get bored and want to progress their career.'

'When you reach CFO level, you have greater responsibility for people management than for systems,' says Geraldine Matchett, CFO of Royal DSM. 'You build and steer the team that can manage systems so your focus must be on bringing in the right skill sets and providing direction and guidance.'

When a finance team is largely autonomous, the CFO is freed up to focus on developing the strategic priorities of the business and building relationships with the CEO, the board and other stakeholders. Bank of America CFO Paul Donofrio points out that it is a CFO's job to spend a significant amount of time with the senior management team, the board, investors and, if appropriate, regulators. 'You don't spend as much time managing down as one would think,' he says. 'So you need to have a layer of leadership below you who can run the various disciplines.'

Reflecting on his own experiences of leading the finance function, Donofrio says: 'You come into the job with your own biases. And you come into the job with everybody else telling you who's good and who's bad. But you have to figure it out on your own, and that takes time. When you want to change a leadership team, you can't do it all at once, because that's risky. You have to do it gradually. You need to take your time and find the right people as you build your leadership team.'

Approaches to leadership in industry

Every CFO or senior partner in an accountancy firm has his or her own leadership style. For example, Jack McGinnis, CFO of ManpowerGroup, establishes leadership by forming enduring relationships with his teams. 'I like spending time with my teams, leading them and making sure I understand how they do their jobs and that they have the support they need,' he says. 'I think it's really important for people to understand that you were once in a position where you could have been doing their jobs so you understand their work. I did a lot of different jobs when I was coming up in public accounting and while I didn't necessarily have to perform the duties that my teams perform, I worked with people in that space and I understand the job they have to do.'

He continues: 'When the CFO has an accounting background and knows the core accounting processes and audit activities, it can be easier for the finance team to identify with them because they know their job is valued.'

A CFO's credibility with his or her team is particularly critical in a large organization, where the CFO may not be able to spend much time with individuals on a one-to-one basis. 'Finance departments are big departments in multinational companies,' notes McGinnis. 'So when people know that the CFO gets it, understands what their job is and what needs to happen in the finance function, that can really strengthen the level of teamwork. It is also important that they feel the leader of the team is committed to driving their career development and giving them the support they need.'

Donofrio's approach to leadership is to get the people who report to him to have collective ownership of all the issues that affect Bank of America's finance function, which numbers over 4,000 people globally. 'So it's not "Oh no, we have an issue in treasury, that's so-and-so's issue",' he says. 'Actually the issue in treasury is everybody's issue. We all own it together and we all have to help fix it. To get things done well and efficiently, we have to draw on each other.'

As a result, it is vital that the function's leaders communicate well with one another. 'They have to talk to each other about what they're experiencing and they have to share all their issues, no matter how easy or hard it is,' says Donofrio. 'And they have to ask for people's help. People also have to speak up and say: "I can help you with that".'

Ronan Dunne, former CEO of Telefónica UK, says that when he has led finance functions, his overarching objective has been to earn the right to be the business's trusted adviser. 'If you keep sight of that, it helps when you are stuck in the trenches, pulling numbers out,' he explains. 'It sets a context that "we are part of creating the conditions for this business to be successful." So some of the more mundane things that we do are part of earning the right to influence the outcomes of the business and to be regarded as the business's trusted adviser.

'When the finance team understands that it can influence and support the business's success, it becomes easier to get through the challenges of month end, quarter end, year end and internal audits.'

For Ian Kenyon, CFO of Cancer Research UK, leadership means having some humility. 'It's very important to remember that while the CFO is a member of the leadership team, he or she is not the only member of that leadership team,' he says. 'And while the numbers are really important, what is also really important is how you get to the numbers.

'So you need to support others to deliver great results. A great finance professional serves the organisation, understands its commercial drivers, asks the right questions and allows the business to operate. In my mind, my role is first to make certain that we put in place the right things to allow the core teams to do what they're good at doing. At the same time, I need to act as a check and a balance – for example, when it comes to signing off on a deal.'

Kenyon started out on his career in practice as a 'good doer' – getting his audits done on time and to the right quality. He then moved into industry and started to take on leadership roles. A defining moment came when he went to work in France with his then employer, retailing giant Kingfisher. 'When I went there, my French was distinctly rusty. I realised that I couldn't be the doer because I didn't have the technical language skills to be a doer in a foreign language. So I identified the people I needed to hire and the structure I needed to set up. Then I started to learn how to get the best out of my people. That's the way I have developed myself.'

Delegating an outcome to his team rather than a task is the way that Kenyon likes to work. 'I'm not a person who says: "I just need a PowerPoint presentation right now." I like to give the context of what we're doing and why we're doing it. I also like to give my team access to the right people. So I take members of my team with me to a meeting so that they can get to hear about something first-hand rather than through me. When I have meetings with my trustees, very often I'll have some of my team with me. It helps them to understand where the questions come from.'

Around three-hundred people report to Kenyon from across the finance, IT, legal and procurement functions of Cancer Research UK. He practises leadership by walking about and being accessible to his teams. 'I have an open-door policy so I am very available,' he says. 'It's an open-plan office so I sit at a normal desk among my team.'

New to the job?

Starting a new job is never easy and stepping into the role of CFO at a large organization – with all the pressures and expectations that entails – can be very challenging, especially if the organization is in financial difficulty. So a new CFO needs to have worked out a simple strategy to get through the first few weeks before he or she has even stepped foot into the office.

Tilston recommends that a new CFO should prepare thoroughly for the role by doing plenty of background reading. 'If I go into a new role, I look at two books,' he says. 'One is *The First 90 Days* by Michael Watkins, which is about how you diagnose what needs to be done and set plans for taking the organisation and the finance function forward. The other one is *The Solutions Focus* by Paul Jackson, which is a book about trying to get people focused on solutions rather than problems.'

A new CFO needs to listen hard and identify potential courses of action in the early stages of his or her new role, Tilston maintains. 'And if you're going to effect any change, it's got to be evident to people early on that change is going to occur. You can't leave it for six or nine months and then say: "I'm going to change what you're doing." People need to see small changes happening in the first month or two. Otherwise they settle back into their comfort zones and either you won't get change or it will be more difficult to get change.'

Tilston also warns that new CFOs who have functions besides finance reporting to them should not stay in their comfort zone of dealing with financial matters at the expense of getting to know other functions. 'You need to make sure that you're seen by other functions that report to you,' he says. 'You need to spend enough time with them to understand their issues and challenges, strengths and weaknesses, as well as those of the finance function. You also need them to educate you on important issues within their area – for example, cyber security in the case of IT.'

Leadership in professional services

While it is hard to lead a finance function, it is possibly even more challenging to assume a leadership role within a professional services firm. That is a result of the other partners being co-owners of the business rather than simply employees of it.

'The biggest difference between a corporate and a partnership is if you're a leader in a corporate, when the CFO says "Go left," everyone goes left and they don't question going left,' says Julie Teigland, regional managing partner for Germany, Switzerland and Austria at EY. 'In a partnership, everyone looks around and says: "Should we go left? Is left a good decision? Maybe we should go right?" In a partnership, every partner is equal in some way, so you need to take them with you on the journey more than if you were the CFO or CEO of a large company.'

She continues: 'In the corporate world, you can take everyone with you through your role justification. I believe that's not possible with a partnership. You have to lead by taking people with you and making them feel that they are part of the decision-making process in some way, shape or form.'

The larger the partnership, the greater the challenges potentially, Teigland remarks.

'We have close to 600 partners in the German, Switzerland and Austria region, which means 600 individual leaders whom we want to take with us on the journey. So even if you have the formal authority to say "I think we should go left," you want the majority of them, if not all of them, to be saying: "Yes, I think we should go left, too."'

Leading partners is also challenging because partners are 'an extremely intelligent, extremely entrepreneurial group of people by definition', according to Teigland. 'If you're trying to lead the best, you know that their ideas are just as valid, if not more so, than your own.'

The fact that professional services firms tend to rotate their leaders presents additional challenges and opportunities. 'You might be a leader today but you might not be the leader in three years' time,' Teigland points out. 'Yet you're giving the input. That's what makes it tough. On the other hand, that's what makes it so exciting!'

Rachel Campbell, global head of people, performance and culture at KPMG International, was just thirty-six when she became a board member of KPMG in the UK. At the time, she didn't quite realize the enormity of her situation – the fact that she was taking on a senior leadership role. 'I had only been a partner for a handful of years when I became a board member so I was quite naïve,' she says. 'It is quite different to be on the board of the firm as opposed to a partner at large.'

She continues: 'Other partners start to look at you slightly differently and treat you slightly differently because you're "in management." Soon I realized that people were "managing" me in a way that they hadn't before. Also, the role sometimes brings conflict because you have to take decisions that you know are going to be difficult for the partners. It's a very different feeling when you're the one who takes the decision versus the one who lives with the decision. But because I've been in a management role for most of my partner career, it's something that I've got used to.'

Campbell's awareness of the yawning divide between those partners who are in management and those who aren't means that she tries to be really accessible to all the partners in the firm. 'If those lines of communication close down, the leadership job becomes really hard because you can't do it without your fellow partners.'

Setting the right tone

'The fish rots from the head,' according to an ancient proverb. This is as true when it comes to leading the finance function as it is in any other aspect of business – or life. CFOs who want their team to follow the highest professional and ethical standards need to follow those standards themselves. It is up to them to set the tone at the top.

'You set the tone and if your tone is wrong, then the tone will be wrong all the way down – unless you are lucky enough to have a very good person in-between,' says Matchett. 'Not having a hierarchical mindset myself, it took me a long time to realise the extent to which people watch what you are doing, what you spend time on and therefore what seems to be important to you. As the CFO, your behaviour sets the tone for the whole function as well as its values – whether you like it or not.'

The CFO is also in charge of setting the vision for the finance function, which will vary according to the strategy of the organization and the maturity of the finance function. 'Your vision may be a finance function that is extremely efficient,' says Matchett. 'So you will be focused on areas such as automation, processes and shared services. If that is the tone that you set at the very top, then people will know that improvements are going to be made in those areas.'

'Alternatively, you may have a very efficient finance function, but one that is disconnected from the company. So here your tone should reflect the need for the finance function to learn about the organisation and to know what their purpose is. While the function is able to process an invoice in a split second, is that truly enough if their purpose is to make the organisation successful?'

Matchett believes that when setting the tone at the top, finance leaders need to recognize the needs of their people. Only by doing this will they get the buy-in that they need to achieve their objectives. 'When people realise that you are interested in developing them, they are much more excited about making the function really effective,' she says. 'They realise that it's about balancing the two.'

Flying high: The Paul Donofrio story

What does it take to become CFO of one of the world's biggest banks? In the case of Bank of America CFO Paul Donofrio, perhaps it was his military background that made all the difference. A keen sailor, Donofrio joined the prestigious United States Naval Academy at the age of seventeen because he wanted to both serve his country and support himself through tertiary education.

'I had the opportunity to be on the water and fly at the same time and I received a great education,' recalls Donofrio. 'So, it was a tremendous opportunity. The military is probably the only career where you can get an incredible amount of responsibility quickly, at a very, very young age. Almost immediately, you're in control of multi-million dollars' worth of equipment and you take charge of many people and, potentially, their lives. So it's a way to get a lot of responsibility and learn a lot of lessons very quickly.'

After spending six years as a naval flight officer, Donofrio weighed up staying with the military and 'making a career out of it' or doing something different. As he was intrigued by the idea of working in finance, he decided to switch careers and take the lessons he had learned in the military to a completely different environment. So he studied for an MBA at the University of Chicago Booth School of Business and then started a career on Wall Street, working in the restructuring group, and later the healthcare group, of US investment bank Kidder, Peabody & Co.

In 1999, Donofrio joined Bank of America with a remit to start a healthcare group. He then went on to hold a string of senior roles including co-head of global corporate and investment banking and head of global corporate credit and transaction banking. Among his responsibilities were leading the integration of Merrill Lynch and Bank of America from a corporate and investment banking standpoint following Bank of America's acquisition of Merrill Lynch in 2008.

Having established a reputation as a strong leader and an effective manager of teams within Bank of America, Donofrio was appointed the group's CFO in August 2015 – despite not holding an accountancy qualification or having had much experience of managing the finance function until that point.

'I think to achieve a senior finance position, there's no one "right" track,' observes Donofrio. 'You really need to understand, and be able to apply, a lot of different disciplines in order to do this job well. And what you didn't learn during your career, you need to learn on the job. You can learn finance through an MBA or accounting through a CPA, but if you can't apply your knowledge to analyse and understand the business, come to the right judgements, and be able to talk about them and influence others, you're not going to get to a senior role in a large organisation.'

In his role, Donofrio has to be able to relate to the people in his team who have specialized skills, draw on their expertise and knowledge and then apply that expertise and knowledge to the whole organization. 'You need to be able to make a judgement, but you also need to be able to take everybody with you,' he explains. 'It's about getting them to appreciate that they need to change what they're doing, so that we can achieve whatever goal we're going after. You can't do it yourself. You've got to get the organisation to do it.'

While a naval training may not seem obvious preparation for a career in banking, Donofrio believes there are some significant similarities between the navy and large corporates. 'The military is a big organisation, but elements of it are very, very personal,' he says. 'If you work for a multinational corporate or a global bank, you have to know how to work in a large organisation, with lots of rules and hierarchy and politics. But you also need to be able to interact at a very basic and human level with people, with a team, in order to get things done.'

Donofrio credits the communication, influencing and leadership skills that he developed in the military with helping him to succeed in his corporate career. 'People often say, "It's easier to lead in the military, just tell people to jump and they say how high,"' he says. 'But it's precisely the opposite. You've got to get people to follow you and you've got to get people to believe in the mission. Those are the skills that I think are most important if you're going to succeed in a large bank or in business.'

He also emphasizes the importance of empathy, saying that while this skill tends to be overlooked, it is actually a necessity for senior people in business. 'Understanding other people's point of view – and really thinking about it – helps you to a) figure out whether your point of view is right and b) if you're convinced that it is right, figure out how to influence them. You really have to appreciate their issues to be able to get them to follow a new path.'

Under pressure

The CFO of any large company will usually be under a lot of pressure – pressure to deliver to investors, to the board and to the management team. 'Everyone handles pressure differently, but some people tend to obsess about it and the more you obsess about it, the less productive you are at doing what you need to do on a day-to-day basis,' says McGinnis.

'My philosophy has always been to focus on the job at hand. Execute your responsibilities and lead your teams in a way that ensures you're delivering the best possible outcomes to your board and your management. If you do that, you'll do about as well as you can and things should work out.'

Companies in certain industries may come under a lot of pressure at particular times – for example, companies in financial services have been in the spotlight since the global financial crisis while oil companies have suffered as a result of the oil price slump. These macro events create a whole new set of pressures for CFOs who already bear a heavy workload. 'When an industry is under pressure, it is going to influence the regulators of the industry, the board and management, and the business models of organisations within that industry,' explains McGinnis. 'It's hard for people to do what they need to do on a daily basis because they spend all their time dealing with media stories or fire fighting.'

As CFO of Bank of America, which was ranked 26 on the Fortune 500 in 2016, Donofrio estimates that he spends between 25 per cent and 50 per cent of his time either directly speaking to regulators or else managing the impact of regulatory change. Being an executive in a large bank right now is very much a change management role, he explains. 'The financial services industry, particularly the banking part of the financial services industry, has fundamentally changed and it's not going back. So we have to adapt to the practical realities of a lower-risk, lower-return industry by innovating our way to a more efficient customer delivery model.'

Donofrio's advice for CFOs who need to work with regulators is to 'realise that they have a very important job to do – they are focused on making sure that the banking system is safe and sound'. Also, they shouldn't deny that problems exist. 'You've got to admit when there is a problem, you've got to be open, you've got to be transparent and you've got to listen,' Donofrio observes. 'We need to prove to everyone that the industry has changed appropriately.'

Matchett says the greatest pressure associated with her job – which is also what she loves about it – is the fact that 'everything in a company is relevant'. She continues: 'If I look at most people in the company, when push comes to shove, they focus on their part of the story and they ignore the rest as being "someone else's problem". But when you're in finance, everything that happens in the company is relevant because it will have an implication on the results.

'I am CFO of Royal DSM, but I am also a member of the management board. In the Dutch context, it's a two-tier board. There's a supervisory board and a management board. There are four members of the management board and we are responsible for every aspect of the organisation from health and safety on the manufacturing sites, to our environmental impact, to governance, and, of course, going concern. All four members of the management board are personally responsible for the company and will go to jail if the company fails to meet its obligations. Whether I am the CFO or not makes no difference to that.'

Even when the CFO does not sit on a management board, he or she is intrinsically involved in everything, Matchett says, 'How can you go to the market and tell the analysts and investors where the company is going if you're not very, very involved in the business operations and strategy? How do you put together the numbers, not only the actuals but the forecasts, if you don't understand what the company is about and what the businesses and R&D are doing?'

Despite the pressures that come with being a CFO, Matchett acknowledges that she is at least shielded from some of the politics that a CEO has to handle. 'While you're involved in all sorts and all eyes are turned to you when things are not going well, you are a little bit protected from some of the HR and reputational issues that the CEO must handle,' she notes. 'The CEO position is a lonely place to be.'

The pros and cons of being a finance leader

The finance leaders who were interviewed for this book generally agreed that their roles required them to work long hours, including weekend and evening working, undertake a fair amount of travel, cope with a lot of pressure and be 'always on'. For example, Julie Brown, CFO of Smith & Nephew and audit committee chair of Roche, says that the demands of her executive role at Smith & Nephew mean that she needs to do a lot of her work for Roche in her own time at the weekends. During AGM season, she also works seven days a week for an extended period. She is able to cope with her gruelling schedule, though, because she enjoys the work and she is able to go on lovely holidays with her family at other points in the year.

McGinnis points out that one downside of being a CFO is not having the same support network as partners within the professional services firms. 'One of the things about public accounting that is unique and really special is the partnership network,' he says. 'Everyone has dealt with similar issues, whether it's an issue with a client or helping the client to deal with an issue of their own. Everyone has been in that situation and so they are focused on helping others. It's a little different in industry. You don't always have the same level of interconnectedness among leaders.'

Both men and women spoke of the effort they put into maintaining some semblance of normal family life. Donofrio used to make a point of reading the same books as his daughters were reading – 'That's a great technique because when I was travelling, I could get on the phone with them and we could talk about the chapter that we'd read.' Meanwhile, Andrew Bonfield, group finance director of National Grid credits his wife and children with keeping him grounded, which is why he tries to draw a line between home and work. 'I'm always contactable but I'm very clear that work is work and home is home, so that determines what I will respond to and when.'

On the positive side, there is the money of course – CFOs at the world's largest companies usually earn seven-figure salaries – but the other pluses outweigh even that. Most significantly, they are in the front seat when it comes to driving the organization forward. 'I really like interacting with the board and the senior management team, helping to make sure they have the best information available to make business decisions,' says McGinnis. 'One of the greatest responsibilities of the finance team is to make sure that we're giving them the best possible financial data, analysis and recommendations. I love that part of the job.'

Senior finance professionals also get exposure to the types of experiences and individuals that other people can only dream about. They get to take big decisions, commit large sums of money to potentially game-changing projects, meet politicians and sometimes even hit the newspaper headlines. Essentially, finance leaders have the opportunity to make a difference in the world. As Donofrio puts it: 'It's a very exciting job where you can make an impact on people's lives.'

Making corporate history

Andrew Bonfield, group finance director of FTSE 100 UK power transmission network National Grid, has found that his accountancy qualification has been his passport to exciting opportunities during a long, colourful – and sometimes turbulent – career.

After qualifying as a chartered accountant with Price Waterhouse (now PwC) in South Africa, he came to the UK as an ambitious 23-year-old in 1987, together with his wife and young son. He joined FTSE 100 pharmaceutical company SmithKline in 1990. There, he rose rapidly through the ranks until he was appointed the company's CFO at the tender age of thirty-six.

He puts his fast ascent to the top finance job down to his problem-solving ability – 'I had solved a few problems at SmithKline and I had a reputation for solving challenging issues' – as well as the fact that the CEO wanted to make an internal promotion.

In addition, there were a couple of significant personal attributes that contributed to Bonfield's success. First, he has the ability to take a step back, look at the big picture and keep issues in proportion. Second, he focuses on the fact that his role is to serve the shareholders' interests rather than protecting his own interests.

It was fortunate that he has these attributes because a year into his role at SmithKline, he learned that the business was going to merge with another pharmaceutical company, Glaxo, with the result that he would be out of a job. 'I had to go through a set of merger discussions where I was not going to be part of the new company,' he recalls. 'That was hard and it was a learning experience having to go through it. After the merger discussions, senior bankers from the other side came up to me and said: "You did a great job." That stuck with me. I did the right thing and later I benefited from doing the right thing, so I will continue to do that.'

The benefit was almost immediate because, following the merger, Bonfield was appointed executive director of finance at another FTSE 100 company, international energy company BG Group. 'One of the first things that people look for when they're hiring a CFO is whether the candidate has FTSE 100 experience,' explains Bonfield. 'So once you've been blooded, you should be able to get another job unless you really, really messed up.'

Next, he became CFO of US pharmaceutical company Bristol-Myers Squibb. While the differences between US and UK accounting standards can act as a barrier to CFOs moving between the two countries for jobs, Bonfield was able to land the Bristol-Myers Squibb role because his background in the pharmaceutical industry was deemed to more than make up for his lack of technical knowledge of US accounting.

Unfortunately, after six years at Bristol-Myers Squibb, Bonfield found himself facing the most common career threat to CFOs: a new CEO. He mentally prepared himself for the fact that he might soon be looking for a new job. 'The CEO got replaced and I jokingly said to the head of HR, "Who leaves first, you or I?" In the end, we both left on the same day.'

It seems that being philosophical is the only way to survive the brutal uncertainty that comes with holding a senior finance role – that, and not falling into the trap of taking the job for granted. 'You know it's going to happen, it's part of your job,' says Bonfield. 'That's what you're paid for and you've got a contract to protect you if the job goes. What's more important is making sure you don't fall asleep on the job because complacency is your biggest enemy. If you assume that everything that goes well is down to you doing a good job, and you're not aware of what could go wrong, then potentially you are setting yourself up for failure.'

Next, Bonfield returned to the UK and took up the job of CFO at confectionary group Cadbury. Almost immediately he found himself plunged into the controversy surrounding the hostile takeover of Cadbury by US food giant Kraft. Politicians and the media treated the takeover, which involved an iconic and much-loved UK company, as a national tragedy. Bonfield points out, however, that the majority of Cadbury's shareholders came from the United States and were always going to make an impartial decision.

'There was a lot of emotion associated with the takeover within the company,' recalls Bonfield. 'But I was probably the least emotional person because I hadn't been there that long and I knew that my job was to maximise value for the shareholders. I thought we fought a very good defence. There are people who say we could have sold it for more, but that's nonsense.'

In 2010, Bonfield joined National Grid as finance director, overseeing both the finance and procurement functions. Around six hundred people report to him across both the United Kingdom and the United States. He normally spends around a week every month travelling in the United States.

It is comparatively easy for a CFO to move between industries, says Bonfield, although different sectors present different challenges from a financial point of view. 'For example, in a regulated utility, your revenue is set in advance so you need to focus on managing your cost base. Whereas in a pharmaceutical business it's more about how you drive long-term value through investment in research and development.'

Despite the dramas that come with being a CFO, Bonfield really enjoys his job. 'There are a lot of benefits to being a CFO,' he says. 'Obviously you build a very close relationship with the CEO and you become a trusted advisor. You are helping to advise and set the course of the company. And you are very influential in deciding how the company operates. You are responsible for a lot of the direction, but you don't always have to take the pressure of making the final decision. That responsibility rests with the CEO. Having said that, I have put myself out there to be a CEO in the past because I would love to take the ultimate responsibility.'

Chapter end

What are the key takeaways from this chapter?

- A good finance leader builds a strong team, develops that team and delegates to that team.
- New CFOs need to start making changes early on in their role so that the finance function knows things are going to be different in future.
- It is the role of the CFO to set the right tone at the top and make sure that the finance function understands what his or her expectations are.
- In practice, a leader needs to be able to bring the other partners with him or her on the journey.
- Being a CFO is a pressurized job, but if you get obsessed about the pressures, you become less productive.

Chapter 6

Women in finance

The secret to my success

'I'm resilient and I don't give up.'

Julie Teigland, regional managing partner for
Germany, Switzerland and Austria, EY

The secret to my success

'I've got a real learner mind-set. I like to try to adopt an approach that means
that I listen and ask questions more than I share what I know.'

Rachel Campbell, global head of people, performance
and culture, KPMG International

If you're a woman working in finance today, you have two major reasons
to feel positive. First, women tend to enter the finance profession in
roughly equal numbers to men, so at the early stages of your career, you
should have plenty of female – as well as male – company in the workplace. Second, finance apparently offers the best route to the top for
women who have ambitions of making the boardroom.

According to a 2012 report from the UK's Cranfield School of
Management,[1] commissioned by ACCA and the Economic and Social
Research Council, women who have a financial background are more
successful than other women in attaining executive roles in FTSE
companies. The study found that nearly half (45 per cent) of female
executive directors were financially qualified while 65 per cent in total
had a financial background. In contrast, just over a quarter (26 per cent)
of their male colleagues were financially qualified and 44 per cent had

a financial background. The three groups of people who were inter-viewed for the research – executive search consultants, chairmen and women who had made it to the board – thought that having a back-ground in the finance function helped women to progress to the top of corporate organizations.

'Finance *is* an excellent career for women,' insists Geraldine Matchett, Royal DSM's CFO. 'It's a profession where you have a serious set of skills in your hands that can really add value to the organisation. You would be surprised by how few people have those skills in most companies. The general level of financial knowledge in most companies is poor, really poor. When you get beyond the P&L and some parts of the balance sheet, and start talking about cash generation, return on capital, etc., many people become uncomfortable. If you have strong financial expertise and can apply it in a constructive way, you find that very quickly you get the respect of the management team around you.'

Nevertheless, while finance appears to present a better route to the board-room than many other professional backgrounds, women are still severely under-represented at the most senior levels. Some of the women who were interviewed for this book talked about what it was like to be 'the only woman in the room' at industry events or to double the number of women present simply by turning up. In February 2015, research by *Fortune*[2] found that men held nearly 90 per cent of Fortune 500 CFO roles – just fifty-eight of Fortune 500 CFOs were women at that time. The picture was similar within the FTSE 100 around that period.[3] At PwC, the world's largest accountancy firm, women constituted 15 per cent of the partnership in 2016, even though they represented half of its global workforce.[4]

The implication of these statistics is clear: while women are attracted to a career in finance and choose to enter the profession in large numbers, they appear to face barriers to progression along the way that prevent them from reaching the top. Unfortunately, progression is not the only barrier that women face. They are also affected by a significant gender pay gap. A salary survey[5] conducted by the Institute of Chartered Accountants in England and Wales (ICAEW) and executive search firm Stott & May in 2015 found that male chartered accountants in business earned an aver-age salary of £100,900 compared with female chartered accountants who earned an average of £63,900. The pay gap appeared to be particularly pronounced for women aged over forty-five, which could be an indicator of the challenges that women face in the profession as they age. Women aged over forty-five saw their salaries drop by £6,500, on average, from the previous year, despite men in the same age category seeing their pay packets grow by £4,200. The research found that the pay gap was narrowest among chartered accountants under thirty. In a statement released to accompany the research, ICAEW partly attributed the gender pay gap to demographics and the working situations of men and women. It said: 'Men are more likely to work in senior roles, the private sector and in regions where salaries are typically higher. Women are more likely to work part-time and in public or not-for-profit organisations where salaries are typically lower.'

'We see a lot more of our male members go into financial services once they have qualified,' observes Sharron Gunn, ICAEW's commercial director, 'and we see our female members pick charities or public-sector organisations. So what appeals to them is clearly different.'

Part of the problem with pay also appears to relate to self-confidence: women are simply not asking for what they are worth. Research by the Association of Accounting Technicians (AAT)[6] in 2016 discovered that men and women who are working in finance tend to have very different ideas about what they should earn. While the men in the study who worked full-time were already earning around 18 per cent more than their female peers, they still thought their pay packets fell short of what they should be taking home by nearly £12,000. In contrast, the women wanted an average of just over half that amount – £7,000.

Furthermore, the study found that men are more likely to push for a pay rise than women. They were also more likely to get one. Over one in four men working in finance (26 per cent) had asked for a pay rise in the previous year compared with less than one in five women (18 per cent). Overall, three in five women (61 per cent) had never asked for a pay rise, compared with 54 per cent of men. Nearly half of the men surveyed (47 per cent) had received a pay rise during the previous year, compared with 40 per cent of women.

If gender is already an issue for women, then background can complicate the situation further. Women from non-white backgrounds report not even being considered for jobs on the basis of their names. A study by headhunting platform Nottx.com[7] in 2016 found that a quarter (23 per cent) of professional women in the UK with 'non-white' sounding names had changed their name to sound more 'traditionally British' in order to get a job. Furthermore, nearly four-fifths (78 per cent) of women felt both their gender and ethnicity were barriers to employment. Men were less likely to change their names than women, but 56 per cent of men still felt they had been discriminated against because of their ethnicity. Worryingly, nearly all (97 per cent) those respondents who did change their names when applying for jobs reported a higher level of call-backs from potential employers compared with those who made applications under their legal names.

Old boys' club

While things are changing – and there is general awareness among both companies and accountancy firms of the benefits that both gender and ethnic diversity bring – today the highest levels of finance are still an old boys' club to some extent. Unconscious bias – the tendency for people to recruit in their own image – means that people who do not belong to the 'right' gender, ethnic group or socio-economic background often rightly feel that the odds are stacked against them in the workplace.

In reality, while organizations appear to comply with equality legislation and draw up lengthy HR policies to that effect, many finance profession-als continue to suffer discrimination on a regular basis. Research by the consultancy Talking Talent in 2014 found that nearly half (43 per cent) of female accountants had experienced prejudice and discrimination in the workplace. The worst culprits in this, perhaps surprisingly, were junior male colleagues who appeared to be trying to assert themselves in a competitive culture.

Men can also unintentionally exclude women in the workplace through the cultural references and language that they use. The use of sporting references (soccer or rugby) or military references in a work context can be very puzzling to women and can put them at a disadvantage because they may be afraid to admit that they don't understand an analogy that is apparently obvious to their male peers.

The way that the modern workplace itself is constructed also serves to discriminate against women. Despite a growing trend towards flexible working, many organizations continue to have cultures of presenteeism and expect their employees to stick rigidly to their working hours. Alternatively, they may expect staff, particularly staff with responsible roles in critical functions such as finance, to put in considerably more hours than their employment contract specifies.

Even in organizations that are supposedly more flexible – the large accountancy firms have flexible working policies, for example – staff typically work long hours, taking calls early in the morning and working late in the evening and over the weekend in order to meet the needs of clients. In big companies, finance is also a long-hours culture – particularly at month and year end – with the time commitment intensifying the more senior someone gets, so CFOs can find that they are effectively always 'on call'.

Given that women usually have the bulk of caring responsibilities in the family, it's not surprising that the time commitments involved in holding a very senior role in finance – either as a CFO or a partner in an accountancy firm – seem unattractive to them. Hence, while men in finance start to take senior roles in their thirties and forties, women's careers tend to fall back into second gear as they wrestle with the challenge of juggling the execution of a ten-digit corporate merger with homework, ballet lessons and soccer practice (and possibly marriage counselling, on top).

It is at this point in their careers that many women take part-time roles – roles that allow them to balance their family and work responsibilities to some extent, but which unfortunately tend to kill off any chances they may have had of ever being appointed CFO. The CFO role is a very consuming one – as is the role of the partner in a large accountancy firm – and people who work part-time are unfortunately still regarded as 'less committed' than their full-time peers. While a period of part-time working may only be temporary for many women, the problem is that it falls at a crucial period in their careers – the point at which they would otherwise be joining the queue for more senior roles.

Of course, not every woman – or man – wants to become the CFO. Some are very happy to get to a certain point and stop. But, for others, the choice is effectively made for them. There is a reason why many of the women who have made it to the top in finance either don't have children or have husbands who don't work or have allowed their career to take a back seat so that they can take care of the family.

Given that comparatively few women hold really senior jobs in finance at present, another obstacle to women is the lack of role models. Since women at the junior and middle ranks of the profession rarely see other women who have made it to the top, they may lack confidence that it will be possible for them to do likewise. Progress is being made in this area through the work of organizations such as the 30% Club, a UK organization that aims to increase the number of women on boards. The 30% Club set up a mentoring scheme[8] in conjunction with EY to offer cross-sector mentoring to women at every career level. Under the scheme, seasoned professionals – both men and women – mentor high-potential women who are able to discuss the challenges they face in confidence and benefit from impartial advice. The scheme has also helped the mentors themselves to understand the issues that women in their own organization are likely to face.

Strategy for success

So if you're a woman who has ambitions of making it to the top in finance, what can you do to increase your chances? The first thing – and it can be something that many women struggle with – is to believe in yourself and in your ability to reach the top. A cross-border study[9] published in the *Journal of Personality and Psychology* in 2016 found that in every country studied, men reported higher self-esteem than women. Interestingly, being a woman in a developed, liberal market where lots of opportunities theoretically exist did not seem to significantly boost women's self-esteem since the confidence gap between men and women was actually narrowest in countries that rank low in gender equality.

Self-belief might be a problem for women, but unfortunately if you don't either have self-belief naturally or make an effort to develop it, then you are crippling yourself before you've even started. Why? Well, if you don't think that you deserve that substantial pay rise or exciting promotion, why should anyone else? As the pioneering American industrialist Henry

Ford is reputed to have said: 'Whether you think you can or whether you think you can't, you're right.'

It is not just enough to believe you can do it, but you also need to believe that you want to do it and that you will get the rewards you are looking for from the effort you put in. Julie Teigland, a senior member of EY's leadership team in Europe, the Middle East, India and Africa, says: 'You have to want it. And we need more women who want it. Is it hard to be in a professional services firm as a partner and a woman? Yes it is.'

If you want to develop your self-belief, you need to start by making a conscious effort to surround yourself with positive people who support you. Where possible, choose your boss carefully because your line manager has an important role in championing you to other people in the organization and in making good developmental opportunities for you. Coaching and neurolinguistic programming (NLP) courses can also help you to increase your self-esteem.

Sacha Romanovitch worked her way through the ranks of Grant Thornton UK to eventually become its CEO. Like many other women, she admits that self-belief does not come naturally to her. 'My greatest challenge is trying not to listen to the voices in my head that say I'm not good enough and I can't do it,' she says. But recognizing that confidence and resilience are crucial components of leadership, she has taken action to enhance her self-belief over the years. For example, she certified as an NLP practitioner and also completed the High Performance Leadership Programme at the Chicago Booth Business School. 'All the neuroscience tells us that you need to give your brain confident instructions about things,' she says, adding that women need to ensure that when they assess their performance in any given situation, they focus on what went right as well as what went wrong.

Mentoring can be another good way for women to work on their self-belief. Your workplace may have its own internal mentoring programme in place, but you may also be able to access mentoring through your professional body if you are a member of one. Both the American Institute of CPAs and ICAEW have mentoring programmes, for example. Networking groups can also be a good way to find mentors. The Australian women's networking group, Women in Banking and Finance, has its own mentor programme – as does the New Zealand Business Women's Network.

Alternatively, if you cannot access a formal mentoring scheme, you might want to approach professionals whom you admire and ask them if they are willing to act as your mentor on an informal basis. You are likely to need different mentors at different times of your career depending on the support you require at any given point. Later on in your career, you should also think about acting as a mentor to others because supporting up-and-coming accountants is not only a way to 'give back' to the profession, but it also enables you to improve your communication and management skills while learning from someone who has a different perspective on business challenges.

Julie Brown, CFO of Smith & Nephew, has benefited from both formal and informal mentoring throughout her career. She was fortunate to have supportive line managers who saw the potential in her and exposed her to new opportunities. She also had the opportunity to work with an excellent management coach. 'He was also a very good sounding board,' she explains, 'because the more senior you get, the more complex the challenges. So it's useful to have an external sounding board that can help you through a situation. He was really good at dissecting problems and making me see the problem from an external perspective.'

Today, Brown sees mentoring her team and talent development as a big part of her role. 'I think about my direct reports in terms of succession,' she says. 'It's one of the best ways of continuing the growth of the company. I'm constantly thinking about potential successors and the skillsets they need to be in a strong position to be the successor. In the majority of the previous roles I've done, I've been replaced with an internal successor, which I think shows it works.'

Torn between work and home

Many women find the period when they are balancing a career with child-rearing a particularly challenging time in their lives. Lydia Lamdin, ICAEW's head of professional development, points out that finance professionals who hold a client-facing role in a large professional services firm are 'pretty much at the beck and call of their clients'. So it can be difficult for them to manage their obligations to their clients with their other responsibilities at home.

While flexible working is becoming an increasingly popular trend, many women are not in a position where they can take advantage of it. So some choose to drop out of the workforce altogether for a while and take an extended career break. The prospect of then returning to work at a later point, particularly to a job that involves a reasonable amount of responsibility, and where the skills required to do the job have changed, can be very intimidating.

Fortunately, employers are increasingly recognizing this, which is why they are launching return-to-work programmes for employees who have been away from the workplace for a while. For example, EY has 'Reconnect', a 12-week programme that gives former managers who have been away for between two and ten years access to training, coaching and mentoring as well as work on live projects with the opportunity of a permanent position on completion of the programme. Deloitte and PwC have similar schemes, as do the investment banks Goldman Sachs, Morgan Stanley and Credit Suisse. The nature of the schemes varies by organization and by geography.

Nevertheless, it is important not to pretend that it is easy to return to work after an extended career break that encompasses a number of years. 'Don't give up but if you find yourself in that situation, you are going to have to be as flexible as you can be about your re-entry into the profession,' says Karen Young, director of Hays Senior Finance. 'It's not always easy to re-enter in the same capacity as you left.

'You may need to take a downward step to get back in, but after six to 12 months you can get back to where you want to be and move ahead. I've seen this progression happen very quickly if someone is prepared to be flexible and take a sensible, entry-level role first.'

Young says that people looking to re-enter the workforce after a period away need to make sure that they are keeping up to date with changing trends in the profession by doing their CPD, reading industry publications, attending events and talking to people. She adds: 'Try and hold down a relevant voluntary position, such as a non-executive directorship or treasurer for a charity while you are on a career break, just to keep your hand in.' She also advises looking for jobs by working with recruiters as well as by making applications directly to employers and drawing on personal networks.

Need to network

Networking is a critical skill for any woman – or man – who wants to get to the top – and that means networking with men and women, both internally within your organization and externally with people from other organizations. The higher you want to climb in your career, the higher your profile needs to be within your industry and the finance profession more broadly. If you want to hold the top finance job one day, you need to start capturing the attention of your peers, managers and executives from early in your career and you need to make strong connections with recruiters, headhunters and those individuals who can make a big difference to your career as it progresses, such as auditors and bankers (if you are in industry) and the key finance personnel who work for your clients (if you are in practice).

As we discussed in Chapter 3, networking covers a vast range of activities – not just the formal situations that we think of as 'networking'. Ideally, we should all be working at strengthening our relationships with our networks each and every day. Nevertheless, if you have had limited experience of networking outside your current organization, women's networking groups can be a very good place to start developing your confidence with networking.

Some of the best-known networking groups for women include City Women's Network and ICAEW's Women in Finance Network in the United Kingdom, the European Professional Women's Network, the Financial Women's Association and the Women's Public Finance Network in the United States, and the Women in Banking and Finance network in Australia. If you enter 'finance networking group' in your internet search engine, you will also find a wide range of networking groups that are open to individuals of both genders. Perhaps the best known is the Financial Executives Networking Group, which has a number of chapters in the United States as well as eleven international chapters, including chapters in Europe, the Middle East, Asia Pacific and South America.

If you really want to succeed in finance, you will need to network actively with key people of both genders during the course of your career – it is impossible to overstate this point. 'It's important that women are networking in the real world,' observes Romanovitch. 'Over the years, I've been to numerous different women's networking events. They're great in the early stages of your career in terms of building your confidence by going into rooms of people you don't know. But given we have limited time to devote to networking, it's really important that we're in the main-stream, connecting with it and changing it.'

Romanovitch also emphasizes that it's not just whom you network with, but also how you go about it that's important. If you attend networking events with the sole aim of meeting someone who can offer you that next big promotion, you will almost certainly end up coming across badly while also neglecting a number of very interesting people who could be beneficial to your career in subtle ways. Also, networking should not just be about overtly fulfilling your own career ambitions. It should also be an opportunity for personal development – a means of deepening and nurturing your knowledge bank – and an opportunity to build and enhance the careers of others by enabling individuals to make connections.

'I've been good at networking throughout my career,' Romanovitch says. 'But it wasn't networking to get something; it was networking because I was curious and wanted to find things out. So I do have a lot of good connections and networks and they gave me some really good ideas and insight into what we could do to develop our business. Then I got really good at sharing and communicating those ideas, which made my part-ners feel confident about giving me the CEO job.' For Romanovitch, networking was a way for her to create value and be seen as valuable to others. 'That's what you need to do. Rather than focus on how you can get to be CEO, think about how you can create value and keep expanding on that value. That's what makes you compelling to other people.'

Being female can be an advantage ... so use it

Something else that women need to tap into as they progress in their careers is their own femininity. While finance continues to be dominated by men at the highest levels, being a woman can actually be an advantage for a number of reasons. First, senior women stand out more because there are fewer of them, so the more senior you are, the more you will stand out. If you are wise, you will use this to your advantage by making sure that people remember your name when they meet you at networking events and by being a good role model to younger women in your team, encouraging them to stick with the organization and do outstanding work – thereby making you look good.

As a woman, you are also likely to benefit from the increased focus on diversity within the corporate world. Numerous studies show that companies with more women on boards perform better, and with more countries adopting quotas to force companies to take on female board members, women will find interesting opportunities if they are ready to go out and seize them. There is also likely to be a greater focus within organizations on bringing high-potential women up through talent pipelines.

As the female CEO of an accountancy firm, Sacha Romanovitch realizes that she is in a position to make more of a difference than her male peers – both to the way women are perceived in the workplace and on other issues. 'I get more of a platform than a man would get as CEO of Grant Thornton UK,' she says. 'But that comes with a sense of responsibility. If you're given more of a platform, how are you choosing to use that platform in a way that changes things differently in the future?'

For example, one thing that Romanovitch is adamant about is that she doesn't want to talk only about diversity issues to the media. Yes, she will talk about diversity, but she also wants to cover other issues. 'It's a problem if every time a journalist speaks to a woman in business, they just want to ask them what it's like being a woman in business. If we let them get away with that, we are pandering to the view that our voice on business isn't relevant or interesting. And that actually becomes part of the problem.'

As a leader, Romanovitch also wants to challenge the popular assumption that leaders are perfect and have all the answers. 'Guess what? We're not and we don't,' she says. 'One of my missions is to try to showcase that we're not and we don't and that's ok. Also, not only is it ok; it's a good thing. Trying to pretend that you have all the answers and you're perfect has led to some awful things happening in the City and elsewhere.'

Although Teigland was born in the United States, at the time of writing she was regional managing partner for the Germany, Switzerland and

Austria region at EY. She believes that one of the reasons why she can be so honest about what she thinks is because she's a woman and she's not from Europe. 'I think it's easier for me to be a woman,' she explains, 'because I can catch people off-guard. I don't know if it will always be like this, but being a woman does provide a level of freedom from some current social norms.'

Teigland is EY's Europe, Middle East, India and Africa sponsor for the firm's Women. Fast forward programme. The programme is aiming to speed up women's progress in the workplace so that gender parity can be achieved sooner. She is also the key driver behind one of the programme's main initiatives, the Women³. The Power of Three forum. This forum brought together leaders from business, entrepreneurship and government to find practical solutions that support the economic advancement of women and made five key recommendations in a white paper released at Davos in January 2016.[10]

The five recommendations were that there should be a global employer of choice awards scheme to recognize employers with programmes that support the advancement of women; that the visibility of both male and female role models within organizations should be enhanced; that there should be intergenerational hubs that allow young women and more experienced women to exchange knowledge; that a digital platform should be created to link female entrepreneurs with other entrepreneurs, investors, coaches and mentors; and that a digital platform should be built to rank the media according to the level of gender parity that exists within their reporting.

While Teigland is acting as a champion for women more broadly, she also has strong ideas about what accountancy firms can do to develop their female professionals. It's easy for firms to make sure that female accountants develop technical expertise, she says, but they also need to give them great commercial experience. In addition, she says that there needs to be a cultural shift so that women don't perceive their childbearing years as the end of their careers, but merely as a period when their career might dip in momentum a little to accommodate their personal needs.

'We've got to do a lot better job of educating women who are in finance and accounting so that they can take the time that they need or want to take care of their children because it's a drop in the bucket compared with their overall career,' she says. 'They just need to be clear about what they want to do and the profession will carry them through. We need to be better about conveying that message.'

Taking into account the total length of a woman's career span – which will be many decades – Teigland argues that not only is it possible for women to get to the top in finance, but it is also achievable and women don't have to sacrifice their lives to do it. 'Even if you have to give up a little bit for a little while, remember that it's only for a little while.'

How does she do it?

Someone who understands how important it is to want to do your job is Rachel Campbell, KPMG International's global head of people, performance and culture.

Campbell started in KPMG UK's audit function and her first client was Pinewood Studios, which meant she got to see the Batman and James Bond movie sets. She built her career in audit, serving clients in the banking, consumer, retail and telecom sectors and rose rapidly through the ranks of the Big Four firm, making partner at the age of thirty. At the tender age of thirty-six, she was elevated to the firm's UK board as head of people. She then went on to become KPMG Europe's head of people and was named global people leader in 2009, when she was still just thirty-nine.

The nature of her role means that Campbell travels extensively – normally two or three weeks out of four. She takes her first call at 7.00 am and works till 10 or 11 at night. When she's not travelling, she tries to get home so that she can be with her children at bedtime. She's also very disciplined about which telephone calls she will take when she's on holiday.

When asked about how she balances family life with her work commitments, Campbell says: 'I'm a very big believer with feeling comfortable about bringing your whole self to work. Otherwise people don't know the dilemmas that you're wrestling with and the challenges you have. Everybody knows about my kids. They could all tell you their names and they're probably sick to death of hearing about them. And I will miss a management team meeting if something important is happening at home.'

Once she turned up late to a global board meeting because her daughter was playing the role of Tinker Bell in *Peter Pan* and that was understandably something that she wanted to see. 'When I told my boss that I wanted to miss the first day of the board because I wanted to see my daughter as Tinker Bell, he just said: "That's great. You should absolutely do that."'

But she continues: 'My fear is that nine times out of ten a woman – or indeed a man – wouldn't even have asked. I think we have to recognise the importance of being open about the fact that the line between life and work is blurred.'

Campbell believes that just as professionals should be able to expect their line managers to appreciate this blurred line, they should expect their clients to be able to appreciate it as well. 'I think we do our clients a disservice when we think they expect us to be available 24/7 and to miss parents' evenings and school plays,' she says. 'I don't think they do – in the same way they don't want to miss them either. But unless you make it ok to say "I can't do this", then it's hard to create that environment where people think they can be themselves at work.'

According to Campbell, professional services firms are very conscious of the fact that they need to work hard at creating environments that support the progression of female talent, especially as they go through their child-rearing years. This includes making sure that they are sponsored and mentored and that they have contact with female role models higher up in the organization. It is also very important not to see the challenges as being only for working mums. 'Now that I am a partner, that's one of the things I work hard at – making sure that we don't lose sight of anyone who is talented because they may not have sponsors or mentors around them.'

While she does manage to balance a demanding career with having a family, Campbell is honest about the challenges and the sacrifices involved. 'It's not easy because I do travel a lot with my job,' she says. 'And I do miss out on certain activities with my kids, but when I'm in the UK I'll either work from home or take the kids to school. I will always be there in time to have tea and do homework. But it's difficult. There's no denying it's difficult.'

Having a job that involves a lot of travel and takes her away from her family has become even harder as Campbell's children have grown older. This is because when they see her with a suitcase, they are now far more conscious about how long she will be gone. 'They're much more alert to you being away,' Campbell explains, 'and I feel they need a lot more support in terms of school, homework and friendship issues. There's just more that I feel I need to be present for.'

Campbell recalls that when she used to return from an overseas trip, her children used to hide her clothes so that she couldn't go away again. But she has always tried to make her travel commitments an opportunity for learning, and fun as well. 'We have a big magnetic map on the wall and we always go and look at where I'm going on the map. If I'm going to a place that I haven't been to before, they'll get a present. It's getting less effective now because I've been to so many places, but my son could tell you where Chile was on a map, by the time he was four – no problem at all.'

Still, Campbell is keen to point out that balancing work and family is also difficult for her husband, another partner at KPMG. 'I think that if you take the time to ask, there are a lot of working men who would like to be more available at home if they felt it was ok to do so,' she says. In fact, making it acceptable for both men and women to be able to say that they want to take advantage of flexible working policies is something that Campbell feels strongly about. 'I always worry that flexible working can marginalise women in the workplace even more because it tends to be only women who work flexibly. This notion that we want to encourage a more agile, flexible workforce irrespective of gender is very important.'

Ultimately, the reason why Campbell can operate at such a senior level and undertake all the international travel that she does is because she loves what she does. She finds her work fulfilling and it gives her purpose. 'I'm deeply proud of the firm I work for,' she says. 'I love my job and I feel my job is really making a difference and adding value. I think one of the things you really have to build is that connection with what you're doing and to be doing something you really love.'

Her advice to other female finance professionals who have their sights set on senior roles is this: 'Firstly, connect with what you're doing and make sure it really counts. Otherwise I think it will be a very hard life because one thing's for sure – you're very likely to really love your kids. Secondly, be really open and upfront with your colleagues and team members.

Trust your team members to understand the challenges of balancing home and work. Don't hide those challenges away. If you hide them, you set up a barrier between you and work. Then it's very hard to break that down over time. Be very open about the challenges and dilemmas you face and trust your colleagues to understand them. I think very, very, very often they will. Finally, when you have to confront the challenges, always, always, always put family first.'

Networking groups for women in finance

Global

The Financial Executives Networking Group – http://www.thefeng.org/chapters/chairmen_international.php

Australia

Women in Banking and Finance – www.wibf.org.au

Women in Finance – www.womeninfinance.org.au/index.php?id=32

Europe

Professional Women's Network – www.pwnglobal.net

Canada

Association of Women in Finance – www.womeninfinance.ca

Women's Financial Executive Network – www.feicanada.org

New Zealand

New Zealand Business Women's Network – www.nzwomen.co.uk

South Africa

The Businesswomen's Association – www.bwasa.co.za

United Kingdom

City Women Network – www.citywomen.org

ICAEW's Women in Finance Network – www.icaew.com/en/technical/finance-and-management-faculty/financial-management/women-in-finance

United States

Financial Women's Association – www.fwa.org

Women in Public Finance – www.wpfc.com/index.php/contact-us/contact-wpf

Women's Public Finance Network – http://www.gfoa.org/womens-public-finance-network

Chapter end

What are the key takeaways from this chapter?

- Finance offers good opportunities for women, but women in the profession tend to earn less than their male counterparts and they are under-represented at senior levels.
- Women need to take advantage of any coaching, mentoring and sponsorship opportunities that they get – and they should actively seek out these opportunities if they are not readily presented.
- Believe in yourself – if you don't, no one else will.
- Women who want to succeed in finance need to network with both other women and men.
- The years when women have heavy caring responsibilities are a relatively small period of time in the context of their overall career.

Chapter 7

Beyond finance

The secret to my success

'If I had to choose one attribute, I'd say curiosity. Throughout my career I've followed interesting threads, read around what I'm doing and met a lot of interesting people.'

Sacha Romanovitch, CEO, Grant Thornton UK

The secret to my success

'My skill is to see things clearly. I think in business, seeing things clearly is very important. You also have to try and explain things clearly to other people as well. Many people get caught up in the detail.'

Stephen Billingham, board chair and non-executive director

The great thing about becoming a CFO or a partner in an accountancy firm is that it doesn't necessarily need to be the pinnacle of your career. It can actually mark the start of a whole new career.

Let's start with CFOs. As far as internal progression goes, once you've landed the CFO job there is usually only one obvious option open to you – and that is becoming the CEO. The CEO's role is not for everybody, but some CFOs – especially those who have had a lot of operational experience during their career – are understandably attracted by the prospect of being able to captain the ship instead of just acting as first mate.

The finance function has traditionally been a fertile source of would-be CFOs, particularly in the financial services industry where strict regulatory requirements and the complexity of the reporting require CEOs to really be on top of their game numbers-wise. Research by executive search firm Heidrick & Struggles in 2011 found that around 30 per cent of Fortune 500 CEOs had spent the early part of their careers in finance.[1] The second-largest provider of future CEOs was sales and marketing, which provided just 20 per cent. The trend for finance professionals to become CEOs is even more pronounced in the UK where 2016 research by recruiter Robert Half found that 55 per cent of FTSE 100 CEOs had a background in finance.[2]

There are a number of reasons why CFOs make good CEOs. They are already proven business leaders who have managed large teams and usually held responsibilities outside their core area of expertise, such as IT and procurement. They may also have acquired line management expertise in operational roles during their careers. CFOs are likely to have been involved in change projects, particularly projects that involve the implementation of new systems, and often they will have experience of helping to guide the company through a difficult time – perhaps a restructuring of the business, a redundancy programme or the refinancing of a make-or-break loan. For a company going through a challenging period, the CFO is often seen as a safe pair of hands by the board as well as by investors and lenders.

Furthermore, the CFO's experience of being in the boardroom over a number of years, his or her relationships with institutional investors and analysts, and his or her close working relationship with the CEO means that he or she usually has an excellent understanding of the commercial drivers behind the business and a good grasp of how to set strategy. It is worth noting, however, that in certain consumer-focused industries such as retail and fast-moving consumer goods, the CFO's relative lack of sales and marketing knowledge can prevent him or her from landing the top job. Also, by far the most straightforward path to becoming CEO – if you are already a CFO, that is – is being promoted within your own company. While there are instances of CFOs moving to other companies in a CEO role, external appointments are still rare, according to Mark Freebairn, partner and head of the financial management practice at executive search firm Odgers Berndtson.

While internal promotion tends to be the route that most CFOs take to a CEO role, it does not mean that would-be CEOs can simply expect to join a company and then work their way systematically through the ranks until they reach the top. They need to pay close attention to the experience that they are building up during the course of their careers and if they are not getting the right kind of experience where they are, they need to be willing to move to another organization in order to get it. Later on, they may find that holding a non-executive role with another company will also enable them to extend their knowledge base.

Aside from anything else, a move will give them the opportunity to find out how other organizations address issues, manage and remunerate their people, shape their culture and structure themselves from a governance point of view. Since CEOs are charged with setting the strategy for their organizations, it is invaluable for them to have a breadth of perspectives to draw on and experiences that will encourage them to challenge the status quo. If you have ambitions of becoming a CEO and you do not have this breadth of perspectives, it is likely that regardless of how competent you are, you will be passed over for the role in favour of someone who does.

Wanting to become CEO is one thing; making it is something else, however. If you want to convince the board that you are worthy of holding the top job one day, you will have to make sure you lay the groundwork from the minute you take the CFO's job – if not earlier. This means forming a constructive relationship with the current CEO – supporting him or her in public and acting as both a sounding board and a sparring partner in private. It also means being a confidante and taking additional responsibilities off the CEO while excelling in the traditional functions of the CFO – overseeing the company's finances, controlling costs, raising extra funding if necessary and managing relationships with investors and lenders.

CFOs with aspirations of becoming CEOs also need to play close attention to their relationship with the board. If they want to present themselves as potential leaders, they need to be capable of influencing the board in their own right and not allow themselves to be seen simply as the CEO's sidekick. A board that is familiar with the abilities of a CFO, and knows that the CFO has a good understanding of the business, will be more likely to see that individual as CEO material than a board that knows comparatively little about the CFO.

Life as a CEO

The challenges that a new CEO faces will vary according to his or her company and sector. Nevertheless, there is one challenge that all CFOs-turned-CEOs have in common: accepting that someone other than them will be wearing the finance hat going forward.

The best way to overcome that challenge is to have a confident attitude about letting go of your old responsibilities – a job that is made easier if you replace yourself with someone who is at least as good, if not better, at doing that job than you were. Remember, however, that when you're working with your new CFO the worst possible type of CEO for him or her to have is someone who used to be the CFO – you need to give the CFO the space to bring his or her own perspective to the role.

When you're moving up to a CEO role from a CFO position, it also helps if during the course of your career you keep finance at the core of your capability set, but don't let it constitute the entirety of your capability set. Use the fact that you have a sound grasp of the financial basics to free you up to think about other aspects of the business because that's what you will need to be able to do when you're CEO.

As a CEO, you will have the opportunity to wield tremendous influence and, depending on the company you run, to make decisions that could potentially affect the lives of millions of people. Nevertheless, there are good reasons why the CEOs of the world's biggest companies earn seven-figure pay packets – they often have to make decisions that are difficult and unpopular and they are usually singled out and held publicly accountable when their company trips up. No wonder, then, that the CEO's role is sometimes described as the loneliest job in business.

Becoming a CEO requires a whole extra level of stakeholder management, even compared with being the CFO. In particular, managing relationships with the board can be a delicate balancing act. While a non-executive chair can hold the CEO to account and fire him or her if necessary, it is the job of the CEO – not the chair – to run the company. So the CEO needs to be clear about when and how non-executive directors can contribute to the debate. For example, there is little point discussing an issue that management has already taken a decision on. Yet on the other hand, the views of the non-executive directors may be needed to reach a consensus on a different issue. Equally, the CEO needs to set clear boundaries – in a tactful way – with other stakeholders such as investors who have their own agendas with respect to the company. While CFOs do come under a lot of scrutiny – especially if a business is not performing well financially – they are shielded from other politics that go with the CEO's role. So the exposure that comes with holding the highest job in business can come as a bit of a shock to someone who is new to the role.

Ultimately, the CEO role can be a natural progression from the CFO job and many former CFOs make very successful CEOs. The key to success, though, as with every other step on your career journey, is being able to understand the unique qualities that you can bring to the role, what the bigger picture is beyond the financial perspective and what you need to do to influence the stakeholders who will help you to achieve what you have set out to achieve.

The CEO in industry: Ronan Dunne

Ronan Dunne stepped down as CEO of British telecommunications company Telefónica UK in July 2016 after nine years in the role. Born in Ireland, he trained as a chartered accountant with Touche Ross in Dublin. He then held a string of finance, banking and treasury roles before being named CFO of Telefónica UK in 2005. He became the company's CEO in September 2007.

Dunne believes that finance professionals who align their financial competence with the commercial purpose of their organization will be those who rise furthest. They also need to play a role in leading and shaping the organization so that they become recognized as part of the organization's leadership.

Explaining his own success, he says: 'I always had the mindset in my career that I am on a journey. So I am always looking for interesting things that stretch me and help me to develop my knowledge. I think that probably reflects itself in the way my career has developed. I have seen every role as a developmental opportunity and a learning opportunity, not just as a job, and I was always very open-minded about where I might find myself.'

An example of this, says Dunne, was the fact that he decided to study for a corporate treasury qualification even though he already had a good qualification as a chartered accountant. At the time he was working in banking and he saw the treasury qualification as both a way to build knowledge and a networking opportunity. 'The people I was studying with were going to be tomorrow's treasurers,' he explains. 'I didn't need to have a corporate treasury qualification, but it improved the language that I used with treasurers.'

He continues: 'One of things I have found over the years is people invest so little time in their own careers. They expect their employer, or HR, or somebody else, to manage their career. But the only person responsible for your career is *you*. My career has not been a straight line of always successful, but I have always put myself in a position to be lucky. Even though I had no idea I was going to end up as the CEO of one of Britain's biggest companies, I always knew I was going to put myself out there and take every opportunity to do some very interesting things.'

Having been CFO and then CEO of Telefónica UK, Dunne has played both roles in this crucial executive relationship. He believes that an opportunity is lost if the CEO and the CFO operate in a very hierarchical capacity – where the CEO is omnipotent and the CFO is confined to a narrow role of supporting the boss. 'I see the CEO and the CFO as co-conspirators,' he says. 'They each have a critical role to play and it is the balance between the two of them that creates the conditions where a business can be more successful.'

The relationship between the CEO and the CFO is very much a two-way relationship, Dunne says. 'There shouldn't be anything that the CFO doesn't know about how the CEO views the business. Similarly, the CEO should understand the CFO well enough to support them at being really successful in their job.'

The day-to-day life of a CEO is as varied as you would expect of such an outward-facing role. 'Good CEOs spend more time outside the business than within,' Dunne explains. 'You are much more likely to learn about your business outside than inside.'

On an average day as CEO of Telefónica UK, around 60 per cent of Dunne's time was taken up with external meetings and commitments, with the remaining 40 per cent being internally focused. He was wary of being briefed for the sake of it and liked to focus his time on where he could make the greatest impact. 'I was focused on understanding what is the thing I could do, and only I could do, which might be putting an arm around the shoulder of a senior colleague or making a key decision that leads onto other decisions.'

Dunne also devoted 20 per cent of his time to doing community work, particularly with young people. He launched Telefónica UK's Think Big corporate social responsibility (CSR) programme, which helps young people with good ideas to have a positive impact on society while developing vital experience and skills. The programme is important, he says, because it encourages the business to understand its own values and it also exposes Telefónica UK to new business opportunities on the basis that people do business with the brands that touch them. 'It happens to be a personal passion of mine that leadership is about having made a difference so that your impact survives long after you have moved on,' he says.

(Ronan Dunne was appointed executive vice president and group president of Verizon Wireless in August 2016.)

Senior leadership in an accountancy firm

There are many similarities between the world's biggest professional services firms and the largest listed companies. Both sets of businesses operate internationally, earn billions of dollars in revenues and employ tens of thousands – if not hundreds of thousands – of people. In 2015, PwC was the largest professional services firm in the world. It had member firms in 157 countries, notched up $35.4bn in revenues globally and employed 208,100 people.[3] In contrast, US retailer Wal-Mart was the world's biggest listed company that year (although it is controlled by the Walton family, which has a 52 per cent stake, it is also listed). It generated $485.7bn in revenues and had 2.2 million employees in twenty-eight different countries around the world.[4]

There are a couple of significant differences between the big professional services firms and large listed companies, however. The first is that despite the growing popularity of corporate structures among smaller accountancy firms, the six biggest global professional services firms are still firmly wedded to their partnership status. So they are private businesses that are owned by all the partners who have been invited to join the partnership and have bought equity in the business. (Some firms also have 'salaried' partners – professionals who hold partner status but do not have equity in the business and are therefore not entitled to a share of the profits.)

Due to the nature of the partnership structure, all the investors in the business are also effectively the leaders of the business. The word 'partner' conveys an impression of equality, the idea that the views of all the leaders in the business are equally important and respected. To a certain extent that is true since partnerships generally make decisions by consensus, although big partnerships also have hierarchical structures and a senior partner whose job it is to set the vision for the firm, along with a senior management team.

The idea of a partnership of equals is not as relevant to a large listed company. Listed companies usually have leaders who are also investors (executives who have shares in the business, for example), but they will also have a large number of external investors, including individuals, investment companies and institutional pension funds. Some of these external investors will be more influential than others depending on the size of their shareholding, but they will be expected to recognize that the business of running the company is the role of the executive team. In a listed company, it is the job of the board of directors to oversee the executives and hold them to account on behalf of shareholders. In a partnership, it is the rest of the partners who will hold the management team to account.

A second significant difference between listed companies and professional services firms is the way in which they organize their people. Listed companies will employ a wide range of people, with a wide range of abilities, in a wide range of roles, and they will often have just one person in the organization doing a particular role. This means that employees, particularly those who are at a higher level in the organization, often don't have peers in the same role, on the same level, whom they can easily approach to thrash out ideas and find ways to resolve problems. So often they will end up going to their direct line managers.

On the other hand, professional services firms sell the services of their people, so their business model is built on recruiting armies of the brightest and the best professionals and sending them out into the workplace where they can deliver results for the firms' clients. As a result, they have large groups of people who are at the same 'grade' within the firm, whether that's audit senior, consultant, manager, senior manager, director or partner. So they have plenty of peers to consult, network with and learn from as they progress in their careers.

Unsurprisingly, given the differences that exist between the large listed multinationals and the professional services giants, holding the top job at somewhere like EY or BDO is not quite the same as being CEO of General Electric or Shell. Whereas the CEO of a large listed company will be chosen and appointed by the board, the CEO or senior partner of a big professional services firm will normally be the person who is thought to be the best candidate for the job by the partnership. Different firms have different processes for selecting their senior partners. Some make use of hustings and elections, for example, whereas others follow more of a behind-the-scenes process where a selection panel identifies suitable candidates and sounds out the opinions of partners privately. Regardless of the selection process the firm uses, potential senior partners need to get buy-in to their vision from the rest of the partnership. So they need to be able networkers, who are well liked and well respected within the partnership and capable of influencing other people, who may have strong opinions and visions of their own.

Rightly or wrongly, partnerships are renowned for being highly political environments where personal relationships and loyalties matter greatly. So anyone who has ambitions of making it to the very top of the partnership structure – either as a senior partner or as a member of the management team – needs to be mindful of this from the very first day on the job and throughout his or her career. If you get to a position when you want to be considered for the senior partner position and you haven't already built up a credible following of allies, then you have left it too late. Since partnerships are based on consensus, you need to be able to prove that you have been consistently effective at building consensus, reaching out to others and persuading others to follow you.

CEO in professional services: Sacha Romanovitch

In 2015 Sacha Romanovitch was named CEO of Grant Thornton UK, the accountancy firm where she had worked for twenty-five years after graduating from the University of Oxford. While she didn't start out with dreams of becoming a partner in a professional services firm, let alone taking the CEO role, her natural sense of curiosity led to her steadily developing herself throughout her career.

'Following threads' is how Romanovitch describes the journey that took her to where she is today. 'I started in audit and I became interested in how we better served our clients and provided value to them,' she recalls. 'That led me into roles where I was supporting the head of department during a period of change in the business. When I came through to partner, my client base included professional services firms and I was also doing some practice leadership.

'Then I was asked to take on the practice leadership for the London office tax practice. Through that I learned a lot about people and I got very passionate about us needing to do more work with our people across the whole firm. So I was asked to take on the national people role on our leadership board, which was a role that hadn't existed before. My journey was very much about following something that felt important, finding out about it, developing it, seeing if it worked, and then putting it onto a bigger stage.'

Romanovitch's remit as Grant Thornton UK's national people and culture leader entailed her looking at scalability and the future of the firm. 'The more I got into that, the more I formed views on where I thought the firm could be in the profession and where I thought it could go,' she says. 'I realised that becoming CEO would give me the opportunity to develop those ideas. So my role has always developed out of the things that felt important for me to pursue at that point in time.'

In 2010, Romanovitch completed the High Performance Leadership Programme at the Chicago Booth Business School. This sparked her interest in the drivers behind organizational success, so she went on to get a Foundation Certificate in coach-mentoring from the European Mentoring and Coaching Council and she gained certification as an NLP practitioner. She also worked with an actor to polish up her public speaking, focusing particularly on 'how to give what the other person needs from your communication as opposed to focusing on what you want to tell them'. Romanovitch has always read widely, both around her work and her clients and around wider trends.

When asked what it takes to be a good leader of a professional services firm, Romanovitch says: 'You need to listen to what's important to people, have a really clear vision of what you think matters and why, be able to share that story and build people's confidence and excitement at delivering it, and be really good at delivering things through other people and bringing them with you on the journey.'

Technical expertise should be taken as a given for finance professionals working in the top firms, Romanovitch believes, so potential leaders need to focus instead on honing their abilities to explain complex ideas to others and on 'drawing out the unsaid'. She adds: 'In any situation with clients or people, are you able to get under the skin of what's really been happening and what's really important? Can you get people to a position of agreement as to what you're going to do and move forward?'

Romanovitch's own development reflects her belief that having strong people skills is absolutely critical in business. 'A lot of the development work I've done is about teamwork and how you work with people to get things done,' she explains. 'How can you extend your horizons of the possible, and how can you effect change in organisations and in people?'

Besides having a natural sense of curiosity and a willingness to invest in herself, Romanovitch puts down her success to having optimism, resilience and a good sense of humour. 'If I don't find something to laugh about every day, then it's all gone horribly wrong!' she says. She also has what she describes as an ability to 'tap into something in people' and help them 'let go of the masks they were holding onto'. This has enabled her to make connections with people throughout her career.

Summing up, Romanovitch says: 'Being able to expand my horizons around what is possible is probably what's made the biggest difference in terms of my success. I tend to explore what's possible and from that make choices and decisions about what we do.'

Non-executive roles

One of the advantages of securing a very senior role in finance, either as a CFO or as a leader in an accountancy firm, is the potential that it offers for individuals to pursue a non-executive portfolio career once they have decided to step back from their executive careers.

Scott Longhurst, group finance director of Anglian Water, also chairs the audit committee of Candover Investments. While his current work commitments mean that he can only manage one non-executive role at the moment, he is interested in building up a non-executive portfolio career (where an individual acts as a non-executive director for several companies) in future. 'One day, I think I might like to wind down a little bit but still spend two or three days a week working with companies that interest me,' he says.

The board of directors is a crucial tool of corporate governance because it is appointed on behalf of shareholders to oversee the company. Large listed companies will usually have a number of part-time independent non-executive directors serving as board members. While independent non-executive directors are paid for their board service, they are not employees of the company. Instead they act in an advisory capacity, which sets them apart from the executive directors who are in charge of the day-to-day management of the company.

It is important to note that board systems vary between countries. In some countries, such as the United States and the United Kingdom, there is a one-tier board system, where both executive and non-executive directors sit on the board. In other countries, such as Germany and the Netherlands, there is a two-tier board system consisting of a supervisory board that comprises independent non-executive directors and a management board that comprises executive directors.

Independent non-executive directors are expected to help executive directors by offering constructive criticism and independent advice in areas such as strategy, performance and resources. Some of their responsibilities include offering a wider view of external factors affecting the organization and perhaps challenging the objectives in the organization's strategic plan, setting the remuneration for executive directors and removing them if necessary. They are also expected to monitor the integrity of the organization's financial information.

The definition of what exactly constitutes an 'independent' non-executive director varies by country. According to the UK Corporate Governance Code, an independent non-executive director should not have been an employee of the company within the previous five years or had a 'material business relationship' within the past three years. A material relationship would include being partner, director, senior employee or shareholder of an adviser or major customer or supplier. This means that a partner in the company's audit firm cannot join the board immediately on retirement. To be considered independent, the director would also have to meet other criteria including not being a participant of the company's pay, pension or pay option schemes. In the United States, a director will not pass the independence tests under the NYSE Listed Company Manual if, within the past three years, an immediate family member has been an executive of another company where any of the listed company's present executive officers simultaneously served on that company's compensation committee.

Often, non-executive careers could commence for individuals when they are holding executive roles. Such individuals may let executive search firms and other business contacts know that they are interested in taking on a non-executive position in addition to their executive role. Acting as non-executive directors for companies other than the ones where they act as executives can give them a broader perspective of the business environment and enable them to acquire valuable knowledge that they can bring back to the organizations that employ them. 'Most large companies are happy for you to do one non-executive role because they get value from you doing it,' says Longhurst. 'They see it as career development and you're bringing experience back into the business.'

Time constraints mean that most sitting executives are able to commit to only one non-executive role. So a portfolio career must usually wait until a later date, once their executive careers have ended. In the case of accountancy firm partners, strict rules around conflict of interest usually mean that they are not even able to start pursuing a non-executive career until they have retired from the partnership of their firm.

Listed companies will typically look for non-executive directors who have experience of sitting on the board of listed companies, although the current pressure on boards to become more diverse means that female candidates may still be credible if they reached one level below main board level during their professional career.

In addition to their professional expertise, non-executive directors are expected to have unimpeachable integrity, an understanding of the business's strategy and the challenges that it faces, the ability to work with – and gain the respect of – other board members and the ability to take difficult decisions in a collegiate manner. At the same time, non-executive directors must be independent and prepared to challenge if they do not support the way in which the company is being run. It is the responsibility of the board chair to ensure that the board works together effectively as a team.

Senior finance professionals who take on non-executive roles tend to find that their analytical skills help them to assimilate and assess the information that they have been presented with. Furthermore, their ability to influence and persuade – skills that they will have honed over the years as a result of being managers and leaders – typically stands them in good stead when they are sitting round the board table.

A good way into a board role for many senior finance professionals is through filling a vacancy on a board's audit committee. Usually, between three and five members of the main board will sit on this committee, which is responsible for making sure that the organization produces accurate and fair financial statements and has robust internal controls and risk management processes in place. It also appoints the company's external auditor and monitors the auditor's performance and independence. Given that current and former CFOs and former accountancy firm partners have a high level of financial expertise and a solid understanding of the audit process, they tend to be highly suited to audit committee roles.

It is not hard to see the attractions of holding a non-executive directorship. Acting as a non-exec can be a good way of staying involved in the hustle and bustle of corporate life without the relentless pressures that come with holding an executive position. Furthermore, finance professionals who have retired from executive life can find that holding a portfolio of non-executive positions offers a healthy income stream as well as an interest.

There is a challenge, however, that comes with being a non-exec when you are used to being an exec – and that is accepting that you need to adopt a different mindset. As an executive, you are part of a leadership team that sets strategy and delivers results for the organization by executing that strategy. As a non-executive director, on the other hand, your role relates to governance rather than management. It is not your responsibility to help run the company; instead, you are there to protect the interests of shareholders (or other stakeholders in a not-for-profit organization). As a result, you will need to challenge management to make sure that they are running the organization effectively and that they have a good handle on the risks involved with the organization's activities – whether these are market risks such as an aggressive new competitor, financial risks such as a high level of debt, or reputational risks such as health and safety practices.

Since a non-executive role involves a big time commitment as well as a legal responsibility (non-executive directors have the same legal duties, liabilities and responsibilities as their executive counterparts), finance leaders who want to take on such a responsibility need to get the support of both the board chair and the chief executive. They also need to do their due diligence on both the company and the board to make sure that the non-directorship is the right fit for them personally and does not present significant reputational risk.

'Be very selective about what you take on,' advises Longhurst, 'because it takes a lot of time and commitment. You need to do a lot of due diligence in order to make sure you pick one that is right for you and gives you the capacity to continue to develop in your day job.'

British Land CFO Lucinda Bell saw a non-executive position on the board of FTSE 250 engineering company Rotork as a good way to extend her 'repertoire of sector experience'. Furthermore, while British Land is a UK domestic business, Rotork operates globally and this – along with the company culture – made serving on Rotork's board appealing.

'I wanted to gain some international experience,' says Bell. 'It was also very important to me to be in an environment where I felt I would be able to enjoy the company of my colleagues. Shared values are fundamentally important to me.'

Bell, who has been with British Land for over twenty-five years, has seen the benefits of holding a non-executive role. 'Having been in one company and one sector for a long time, I've learned a huge amount by being in another sector,' she explains. 'One of the reasons why I chose to go to a company that is smaller rather than larger than British Land was I thought that would give me a bit more visibility of the nuts and bolts of the business.' She acknowledges that being a non-executive means that she has to make 'extra time', but she points out that her commitment to Rotork means that she creates space for her own team to grow since they take on some of her responsibilities at British Land.

As audit committee chair of Swiss healthcare company Roche, Julie Brown has to balance her non-executive board and audit committee commitments with her executive role as CFO of Smith & Nephew. Being Roche's audit committee chair involves attending five or six meetings during the course of the year, which generally take place over eleven to twelve working days.

'But in addition to that you've got all the pre-work,' says Brown. 'You need to read the papers in the lead-up to the meeting. You're responsible for setting the agenda, for looking at all the papers beforehand and for ensuring that they are tailored towards the needs of the committee. And you're responsible for following up on actions and for having meetings with the CFO, the head of internal audit and the independent auditor.'

Non-executive directors need to be diplomatic, but they also need to have analytical capability, the ability to spot issues and to know when to ask the right questions of the right people, says Brown. 'Clearly you have a management team who manage the business and whom you have to enable, facilitate and trust to manage the business, but at the same time you've got a governance role so you have to know when to ask the right questions and probe more deeply.'

While her audit committee chair role is a sizeable time commitment, Brown is glad she took it on. 'There are lots of ideas you pick up as a non-exec that you can apply to your exec career and vice versa,' she says. 'Also, being the chair of the Roche audit committee allows me to see far more how the Smith & Nephew audit committee chair feels. It gives me a level of insight that I wouldn't otherwise have had.'

The board chair's story

In 2009, Stephen Billingham left his role as group finance director of FTSE 100-listed company British Energy after the business was sold to French energy giant EDF for £12.5bn. Wanting a break from what he describes as 'the treadmill of reporting' and the heavy burden of day-to-day senior managerial responsibilities, he opted to pursue a non-executive portfolio career instead. He liked the prospect of having the opportunity to learn new things and being able to work with companies that interested him, while working in a flexible way.

Having set his sights on a portfolio career, he was proactive about making his interest in non-executive roles known. 'You've got to make yourself accessible,' he says. 'You have to make yourself available to head hunters and you also have to network and go out and make contact with people. You have to take long shots at jobs just to remind people that you exist because one of the dangers is when you stop an executive role, unless you are very high profile, people can forget you. You can disappear off the radars unless you put an effort in to ensure you keep selling yourself and that people know your profile. That is very important because you will probably pick up jobs through contacts.'

At the time of writing, Billingham was a non-executive director on four UK boards – utility company Anglian Water, infrastructure group Balfour Beatty, pub owner Punch Taverns and uranium enricher Urenco – and was acting as board chair for all of those businesses except Balfour Beatty. During his non-executive career, he has also served as chair of the audit committee and he believes his finance experience meant he could add particular value in that role.

Billingham emphasizes that becoming a non-executive when you are used to being an executive requires a shift in mindset. 'You have to be conscious of the fact that you cannot turn up at board meetings and try to run the company,' he says. 'At the end of the day, you are not running the company; the management is running the company. You are ensuring the managers are doing a good job.'

He continues: 'You need to pace yourself more than you did with your executive role. You are there to challenge and review. You are not there to just make big things happen. Some people on boards really struggle with the fact that they are not executives anymore.'

Before he goes to a board meeting, Billingham focuses on getting himself into the right mindset by asking himself this question: Who am I today? 'That's a very important question to ask because that gets you in the right frame of mind,' he says. 'There is a danger that as a non-executive you could turn up and think you know all the answers. But that is not the way to do it. You need to make sure you are asking the right questions.'

Chapter end

What are the key takeaways from this chapter?

- If you want to make CEO one day, your best chance of doing it is internally – by being promoted from the CFO job. It is rare for a CFO to be appointed CEO of an external organization.
- Potential CFOs need to win over the board. So they need to convince the board that they will make a good leader in their own right. Broadening out their skill set beyond finance will help them to achieve this.
- In practice, senior leaders need to operate by consensus, so they must have demonstrated the ability to influence and bring others with them throughout their career.
- Once you have stepped down as an executive, it is essential to keep networking with headhunters and business contacts if you want to pursue a non-executive portfolio career.
- Non-executive directors need to do a lot of due diligence when selecting their roles because a directorship is a big time and legal commitment.

Chapter 8

The accountant as an entrepreneur

The secret to my success

'I get things done. In the office, if there was something that needed doing, I did it. I didn't wait until it rose to the top of the pile. I did it within 10 minutes or however long it took till it was done. I did it immediately.'

Peter Hargreaves, founder, Hargreaves Lansdown

The secret to my success

'There is no one thing that leads to success, but I would definitely rank very highly on communication and learning enough so that I can make good decisions.'

Brad Sugars, founder, ActionCOACH

Do accountants make good entrepreneurs? This question tends to prompt heated debate since there is a myth that people who trained as accountants are unsuited to entrepreneurship because they are too cautious and averse to taking risks. In reality, the answer depends on the individual's personality and how much effort he or she wants to put into educating himself or herself to develop the skills that entrepreneurs need.

Many budding entrepreneurs choose to get some kind of training in accounting precisely because they think it will give them a good grounding for running their own business at a later date. Others see accounting as a 'back-up' option. They do the training, start to practise as accountants and then never manage to do anything else. Research by UK job board Careers in Audit in 2007 found that almost a third of accountants had dreamed of becoming entrepreneurs before they started their professional training.[1] (Interestingly, 22 per cent had wanted to become lawyers, 14 per cent had hoped to become sports stars and 3 per cent had set their sights on becoming pilots.)

Entrepreneurship is a hard path for anyone to take, but accountants stand as good a chance as anyone else of making a success of it. Among the well-known entrepreneurs who have a background in accounting are Peter Hargreaves, founder of FTSE 100 financial services company Hargreaves Lansdown, Michael O'Leary, the Irish businessman who was instrumental in building up Ryanair into the leading budget airline that it is today, and Bob Parsons, founder of US domain name registrar GoDaddy.com.

Accountants who work as partners in public practice might also argue – quite reasonably – that they are entrepreneurs. They are owners of the businesses that they run, responsible for bringing in and retaining clients, and innovators who develop new products and services. Nevertheless, there are some fundamental differences between being a partner of an accountancy firm and being an entrepreneur in its truest sense. A partnership, especially a large partnership, offers the kind of security and resources that the CEOs of start-ups don't have, for example. The fact that partnerships are based on consensus also means that individual partners tend to have less independence to make decisions than entrepreneurial CEOs. On the other hand, they also benefit from shared accountability and responsibility when things go wrong.

If we set aside the argument of what actually constitutes an entrepreneur, it is clear that having a background in finance should be a terrific advantage for business owners. Not only does it mean that they have the skills to be able to control the cash flow, manage the costs and raise the funding for any company that they start, they also have the skills to read the financial statements of any other companies that they might want to buy.

'If you struggle to read the financial statements of the companies you want to buy, you can struggle to buy good companies,' observes Brad Sugars, an Australian serial entrepreneur who founded ActionCOACH, a global business coaching franchise network that operates in fifty-four countries. Sugars, who grew up in Brisbane and studied accounting at university, is also a renowned author and speaker. Now a multimillionaire, he is based in Las Vegas.

'Numbers are the language of business so if you understand numbers, you'll understand business,' Sugars explains. 'If you don't understand numbers, you'll struggle with business. Even in sales, you need to talk about numbers. You've got to know margins and you've got to know profit. There's a definite need to understand the numbers when you're in business.'

Nevertheless, while understanding the numbers is crucial in business, entrepreneurs need a whole host of other skills in addition to financial skills. They need to be able to lead; inspire; define the vision; set strategy; attract, motivate and retain good employees; develop, market and sell products and services that other people want to buy; establish systems and processes; and manage their own time effectively so that they don't fall victim to burnout. They also need to have a strong mindset and self-belief because running a business can be tough, especially in the start-up phase or during times of economic uncertainty.

Finally, the importance of being a great communicator cannot be understated because entrepreneurs need to be able to communicate their vision to customers, employees, suppliers and the world at large. 'The ability to communicate as the leader or entrepreneur of a company is vital,' says Sugars. 'Too many companies don't have good sales because they're not good at communication. If you're not good at communication, your business is going to struggle when it comes to sales.'

Dreaming big

New Zealand-born Rich Neal, CEO of financial and audit software company MyWorkpapers, has been running his own businesses since he was in his 20s. A CPA by training, he began his career with Arthur Young (later EY) but left to start an accountancy practice with a colleague from EY. The practice evolved to undertake back-office bookkeeping work and tax returns for other firms. Then, tired of exchanging time for money, he decided to move into the business of providing audience response click-ers that are used at conferences. He launched the business that has since become KeePad and, with some co-founders in the United States, he later launched Turning Technologies.

Like many entrepreneurs, he found the early days extremely tough, however. 'Through the KeePad days and the early days of Turning Technologies I went through a stage where I had no money,' he recalls. 'I had five sons – all babies – and we had to borrow money to buy groceries. I was borrowing money off friends for a year. I can remember my mother-in-law saying to me: "You're just a dreamer. Forget about it and go and get a job. You're a dreamer." My own mother would say the same thing.

'But when you believe in something, and you know it's right, it's like a jigsaw puzzle. You've got to bring the pieces together. You've got to make the business model right. You've got to make your pricing model right. You've got to make your go-to-market strategy right.'

The risk and the effort paid off because by 2007 Turning Technologies was the fastest-growing privately held software company in the United States. Two years later, Neal exited, 'made a bit of money' and started his current business.

Now based on Australia's Gold Coast, Neal still has a keen eye for numbers, but he puts a lot of his business success down to common sense as well as commercial acumen. 'I just say: If this were me as a client, how would I feel? If this were me as a staff member, how would I feel? If this is me as the owner of the business, what am I trying to deliver?'

Significantly, he has also taken steps to differentiate his personal brand as a way of advancing his career. 'One of the earliest tricks I used in my accounting practice was to change my name from Richard to Rich,' he says. 'People remember Rich.'

Education, education, education

While high-performing entrepreneurs tend to need a very rounded skill set, the good news is that it is possible for anyone to acquire this skill set provided he or she is willing to invest in his or her own education by reading business books, attending courses and webinars, and working with business coaches.

Education in business is crucial, according to Sugars, because knowledge is key to making good decisions. 'It's really easy in business to make a decision on less than enough information,' he says. 'If you do that, the business will start to struggle. You've got to be able to get enough information to make a good, solid decision.'

To gain this kind of knowledge, finance professionals who want to become entrepreneurs need to be willing to step outside their comfort zone and get help from others. 'If you want to be successful in business, you have to understand that you're a business person, you're not a finance professional,' Sugars points out. 'So as a business person, are you good enough at sales, marketing, handling the customers and the other aspects of running a business that will determine whether you're successful or not? And you've got to make sure you're building a good, solid business so get some advice on business. Don't just dive in there and think you know what you're doing. You've got to learn how to be a good business owner.'

Sugars' advice to would-be entrepreneurs is to make sure they put together a business plan, not for the sake of the document itself but for the sake of all the thinking and ideas that go into the plan. His other recommendation – which is potentially controversial – is this: 'If you're going to go into business for yourself, go into something that the customers love, not something you like. The whole theory of do what you love is complete rubbish. If you do something you love, you work ten times harder than someone who doesn't do what they love. You work so much more because it's something you love doing.'

How to become a billionaire

If you're looking for an inspirational tale of a finance-professional-turned-entrepreneur, it's hard to beat the story of Peter Hargreaves – arguably Britain's most successful accountant ever.

Hargreaves trained as a chartered accountant in a provincial UK accountancy practice before joining Peat, Marwick, Mitchell & Co (now part of KPMG) as an auditor. He lasted a year in the job before he was sacked, but is sanguine about his dismissal. 'It was absolutely right,' he says of his premature departure. 'I didn't fit.'

Undeterred, Hargreaves went on to hold a string of jobs in industry including roles as a computer salesman for a small business and as an internal auditor for brewer Whitbread. After working in a Bristol-based investment firm for a while, he decided that this was the kind of business he could run himself.

So in 1981 he founded financial investment firm Hargreaves Lansdown with another accountant and former colleague Stephen Lansdown. The business that began in the spare bedroom of Hargreaves' flat is now a FTSE 100-listed company, worth around £6bn, with more than £50bn in assets under management. 'That is enormous,' says Hargreaves. 'We're bigger than most of the building societies were when we started. Our transactions are of the numbers associated with a bank's volume of transactions.'

From the start, Hargreaves Lansdown was a marketing-led operation. The company began by sending out newsletters containing independent guidance on how individuals should invest their money. It then progressed to becoming a broker, selling funds and shares as well as related products via its website and through the mail to UK-based retail investors. What Hargreaves calls 'knock-your-socks-off customer service' was the business's defining feature.

Interestingly, if you ask Hargreaves about the secrets behind his success, he points to his marketing prowess rather than his financial background. Nevertheless, it is clear that financial discipline underpinned the impressive growth of Hargreaves Lansdown. Despite the company's rapid success, both founders paid themselves comparatively modest salaries for many years and they refused to borrow money to grow the business. Investment in the company was funded by profits while the two founders monitored expenditure carefully.

Recognizing that the investment industry can be feast or famine depending on market conditions, Hargreaves Lansdown also built up a large cash buffer. 'We always had enough money in the bank to last a year if we did no business at all,' Hargreaves reveals.

Contrary to many entrepreneurs, Hargreaves believes that business success is not dependent on risk taking. 'In general there's no need for risk in business,' he explains. 'If you're spending a lot of money on something, it shouldn't be a risk. You should know categorically that it's going to come out all right.'

Looking back on his life, Hargreaves is justifiably proud of what he describes as 'an achievement that no one else has ever done'.

He continues: 'That is, to create a FTSE 100 company – in your lifetime – without any borrowing or acquisitions. It's never been done before and it will probably never be done again.'

But while he always thought the business would be successful, even he has been stunned by the sheer size of the numbers involved. 'When we started out, if you were worth £10m you were in the *Sunday Times* Rich List,' he says. 'You're not really rich now unless you've got £100m plus. It's the size of the numbers that I could have not predicted or envisaged.'

Hargreaves himself is now one of the richest men in the world, worth $3.1bn according to *Forbes* and ranked number 595 on its 2016 Billionaires List. Known for his modest life – by billionaire standards, at least – Hargreaves said he was mortified the first time he appeared on a rich list because he had always had the same friends and none of them quite realized how wealthy he was.

While Hargreaves does not believe that accountants make natural entrepreneurs, he says that those accountants who do have an entrepreneurial streak tend to be very successful because their financial nous gives them an advantage. 'Everything revolves around finance now,' he explains. 'Businesses are no longer valued on their assets; they are valued on multiples of profits. So if you understand how money works and you understand the balance sheet, then you are going to be – if you are entrepreneurial – a good entrepreneur.'

Asked for his advice to would-be entrepreneurs, Hargreaves says: 'Look at a lot of businesses, work for a lot of businesses. Find out what makes businesses successful and why businesses fail. You learn more from a bad business than you do from a good one. You learn far more from a failure than you do from success.'

Chapter end

What are the key takeaways from this chapter?

- Having financial expertise can be a great advantage for an entrepreneur because numbers are the language of business.
- Besides financial expertise, entrepreneurs need to possess a host of other skills including the ability to set strategy, develop new products and services, and lead and manage people.

- Educate yourself by reading business books and attending webinars and courses. Be willing to learn from others.
- Put together a business plan – not for the sake of the document itself, but for all the ideas and thinking that go into it.
- Remember, when the going gets tough, that as an entrepreneur you learn far more from failure than you do from success.

Chapter 9

Conclusion

Who do you need to be if you want to become a senior finance leader? From talking to the finance leaders who were interviewed for this book, it is clear that you need to be pretty special.

You need to have a strong and enduring personal brand and to come across as someone who is authentic and acts with integrity. You need to be a skilled and capable technician, as well as a trusted business partner who is able to build effective relationships with a wide range of people – both within and outside your organization. You need to invest time in your team and in helping them to be the best they can be – even if that means that one day they will be better than you are. You need to be committed to educating yourself and to building up a broad and rich base of career experiences. You also need to be capable of spotting opportunities and willing to take the calculated risks that will propel you to the next level in your career.

Above all else, you must *want* to do the job. Being a finance leader requires a huge amount of determination, commitment and personal sacrifice. If it is not a job that you passionately want to hold, you will almost certainly never get to hold it.

To return to a question that inspired this book: Are finance leaders born or are they made? The truth is that they are probably partly born and partly made. What is less clear is how you can know if you were born with the potential to become a future finance leader. Ultimately, it is only by trying to make it that you are likely to find out.

About the author

Sally Percy is a business and finance journalist. A former editor of *Accountancy* and *The Treasurer* magazines, she now runs her own financial content agency Love Letters Publishing – www.loveletterspublishing.co.uk. Follow Sally on Twitter @SallyPercy

© Sally Percy 2017

Notes

Chapter 1

1 *Professional accountants – the future, ACCA, 2016.*

Chapter 2

1 http://fortune.com/2015/05/19/mba-graduates-starting-salary.

2 *The Chief Financial Officer: What CFOs Do, the Influence they Have, and Why it Matters,* Jason Karaian 2014.

3 *The DNA of a CFO,* EY 2016.

4 *DNA of an FD,* Hays 2013.

5 *DNA of a Partner,* Hays 2014.

Chapter 3

1 https://www.roberthalf.co.uk/news-insights/reports-guides/cfo-insights/robert-half-ftse-100-ceo-tracker

2 http://www.russellreynolds.com/newsroom/companies-dont-need-cfos-to-be-cpas-anymore

3 http://www.gallup.com/businessjournal/182321/employees-lot-managers.aspx

Chapter 4

1 *Finance 2020: Closer than You Think,* Robert Half, 2016.

2 *The Robots are Coming,* Deloitte, 2015.

3 https://next.ft.com/content/268637f6-15c8-11e6-9d98-00386a18e39d

4 *The Future of Business: Critical Insights into a Rapidly Changing World from 60 Future Thinkers,* edited by Rohit Talwar, Fast Future Publishing, 2015.

5 *100 Drivers of Change for the Global Accountancy Profession,* ACCA and IMA, 2012.

Chapter 6

1 'Women in Finance; a Springboard to Corporate Board Positions?', Cranfield School of Management.

2 http://fortune.com/2015/02/24/58-women-cfos-in-the-fortune-500-is-this-progress/

3 http://www.financialdirector.co.uk/financial-director/feature/2380725/recruiter-tries-to-bulk-up-women-cfos-in-the-ftse-100

4 https://www.pwc.com/mt/en/about-us/women-at-pwc.html

5 http://www.icaew.com/en/about-icaew/news/press-release-archive/2015-press-releases/salaries-drop-for-experienced-female-accountants-as-gender-pay-gap-widens

6 http://www.aatcomment.org.uk/aat-view/front-page-latest-featured-articles/men-nearly-twice-as-bullish-as-women-over-salary-expectations

7 http://www.recruitmentgrapevine.com/article/2016-04-15-ethnic-women-changing-their-names-in-a-bid-to-find-a-job

8 http://30percentclub.org/initiatives/mentoring-scheme

9 http://time.com/4167501/money-cant-buy-you-self-esteem-if-youre-a-woman/

10 *Who Holds the Key to Closing the Skills Gap?* EY, 2016.

Chapter 7

1 http://www.forbes.com/sites/ciocentral/2011/12/05/the-path-to-becoming-a-fortune-500-ceo/#3455558028c9

2 https://www.roberthalf.co.uk/press/combination-background-finance-and-industry-knowledge-key-success-ftse-100-ceos

3 *Global Annual Review 2015*, PwC.

4 http://corporate.walmart.com/our-story/our-locations

Chapter 8

1 http://www.accountingweb.co.uk/topic/practice/third-accountants-are-frustrated-entrepreneurs

Index

10/17